1.50

M000097292

"Did I Do Something Wrong?"

Sheila + Fred
from
Heidi
May '95

"Did I Do Something Wrong?"

A Supportive Guide for Parents and Loved Ones of People in Therapy

Heidi H. Spencer, Ph.D.

New Horizon Press   Far Hills, New Jersey

Copyright © 1995 by Heidi H. Spencer

All rights reserved. No part of this book may be reproduced or transmitted in any form whatsoever, including electronic, mechanical, or any information storage or retrieval, except as may be expressly permitted in the 1976 Copyright Act or in writing from the publisher.

Requests for permission should be addressed to:
New Horizon Press
P.O. Box 669
Far Hills, NJ 07931

Spencer, Heidi H.
        "Did I Do Something Wrong?": A Supportive Guide for Parents and Loved Ones of People in Therapy

Library of Congress Catalog Card Number: 94-066758

ISBN: 0-88282-128-8

New Horizon Press

Manufactured in the U.S.A.

1999 1998 1997 1996 1995 / 5 4 3 2 1

With love to

David—for his generosity of spirit
Hans—for his wisdom and song
Jason—for his fair-mindedness and courage
Tanya—for her spiritual grace

REFLECTIONS

Tim sat alone—on the living room couch—
Silent, somber.

Mrs. Jasper returned from work.
"What is he thinking?" she wondered . . .
As she tiptoed by.
But she did not ask.

Tim cut the lawn and fixed Dad's car—
Without a word.
"What is Tim thinking?" pondered Dad.
But he did not ask.

Tim's mind was active . . .
       as he pondered who he was
       and where he'd been . . .
       and where he was going.

Neither alone nor lonely as before,
Tim wore the face of reflection.

But no one asked what he was thinking.
No one dared.

Tim was doing his work.

H.H.S.

CONTENTS

ACKNOWLEDGMENTS

This book is rooted in life experience, hours shared with clients, and personal growth within my network of family and friends.

I thank my clients and their loved ones for entrusting their stories and struggles with me. Their universal yearnings form the thematic subtext of this book.

I thank the first readers of this book: my husband, C. David Spencer, M.D., for his belief in my ideas; my mother, Annamarie Kunz Honnold, for her maternal endorsement; Kathleen Kenyon, for her affectionate encouragement; Dorothy McGhee, for her helpful suggestions; Kirstin Romaine Jones, for taking this book to heart; and The Union Institute of Cincinnati for respecting the delicate interface between my personal and professional concerns.

Appreciation also goes to my father, John O. Honnold, Jr., for his practical and legal guidance; to Alison J. Picard, for finding this book its home; to Frances Eddy, for transforming this work into legible form; and to my friends who stood by as I disappeared into my separate space.

Abiding love is sent to my young adult children, Hans, Jason, and Tanya, who keep teaching me how to be both a parent and a person. I will always be grateful for their inspiration, humor, respect, and affection.

AUTHOR'S NOTE

This book is based on both my research and extensive interviews. In order to protect the identity of others, I have changed people's names and identifying characteristics. The conversations portrayed in this book have been reconstructed.

Although, for convenience sake, a specific gender or type of relationship (e.g. parent-child or spousal) is sometimes referred to in the text, most advice contained in this book is directed equally toward males, females, parents, partners (husbands, wives, or significant others), and peers.

PREFACE

Psychic pain cuts through all economic, racial, religious, and gendered subgroups of our population. Although the people I talk about were raised in homes of differing racial, religious, economic, and ethnic backgrounds, I've described their dilemmas in terms of universal human yearnings and problems. By sharing these therapy room communications, I hope to give you the reader a mirror into the innermost feelings of others so that you can see how alike they are to your own feelings. From this recognition will come, I hope, the beginning of finding solutions to problems about which many people in or out of therapy may have wondered and worried.

Throughout this book I use the term "adult child." The English language offers few terms for describing the adult son or daughter. Of course, we can refer to "offspring"—a fitting label for "children" who "spring" away from us as they strive for independence. But this word is awkward.

"How many children do you have?" I ask parents in their sixties, seventies, and eighties. "I have two children—ages forty and fifty," responds one dignified older mother. The word "child" is associated, according to Webster, with a young person whose age typically ranges from infancy to youth.

I use the word "partner" to describe marital spouses as well as people in committed relationships.

There is not an appropriate label for the person who decides to find help through therapy. Clinicians refer to the people they help as either "patients" or "clients." Neither of these terms is fully accurate. The word "client" emphasizes the business dimension of the relationship. The term "patient" implies that the individual is either ill or receiving care. Neither expresses the high level of commitment, effort, and courage required of people in therapy. The success of a completed treatment process depends on the intelligence and initiative of both "patient" and clinician. I have chosen to use the word "client" because it denotes a person who has willingly sought the help of a professional in order to receive sound advice and guidance.

"Health" is defined by Webster as being "hale" or "sound of body, mind, or soul." Most people think of "health" as the absence of pain, but no one is always "pain free." For life, despite its joyous celebrations, is punctuated by disappointment, loss, and constant readjustment. Most of the people you will soon read about are as inherently sound of "body, mind, and soul" as you and I. Perhaps more so.

An old myth implies that people who seek psychotherapy are "sick," "weak," dependent, or deficient. I strongly challenge this myth. Most people I have met in therapy are unusually determined to realize their emotional, intellectual, spiritual, and physical potentials. During psychotherapy, many individuals deepen and clarify their religious beliefs. They may also insist upon attaining physical well-being. Whereas others may take their emotional health for granted, people in psychotherapy work hard to ensure long, productive lives.

Who can really define what health means? Some describe it as the capacity to fulfill one's potential. Others define it as self-acceptance, self-knowledge, or emotional resilience. When we feel healthy, we feel whole, at peace, and emotionally alive. Healthy people can fully enjoy their capacities for work, for play, and—most importantly—for love.

I invite each of you to view emotional health as a relative, rather than absolute, state of well-being. We all have problems. Some individuals' difficulties do not warrant professional assistance. Others, those who are mentally ill, carry enormous psychic burdens which require social and medical support. Most of the people who walk through the therapist's door, however, fall between these extremes: they seek mastery over a set of life challenges or symptoms which puzzle and plague them. They are in pain. With time and effort, their difficulties can be eased, as their resilience is enhanced. They can be revived by their ability to love.

If you are a parent, partner, relative, or friend of an adult in therapy, I hope you can honor yourself for who you are and who you have been. Your loved one in therapy is pursuing the same task. Change takes time. Efforts to be honest with ourselves require courage. I have tried, by sharing the journeys of others with you, to be genuine and clear. What remains unsaid or uncertain is left for you to resolve. Ask your loved ones for clarification. Ask yourself for the truth. Then listen for honest answers.

INTRODUCTION

I've often wished I could meet personally with those of you who are affected by the precarious inner journeys of your loved ones in therapy. Since this has usually been impossible, I've written this book. I view it as a letter of both explanation and invitation. I've written this letter to you, the parents, partners, and peers of people in therapy.

The stories of two of the many people whose concerns prompted me to write this book are:

Jessica

A painfully shy young artist, Jessica requested my assistance because of "relationship problems." One day, excited after an energizing therapy hour, Jess called her mother in Omaha to "talk about therapy." She was sure her mother would be excited about her progress and by the fact she'd been elected President of the Outing Club.

When Jess arrived for her next visit, however, she stared at me through hollow green eyes. Her twinkling vitality had vanished. She told me she hadn't slept for two days.

"It was a mistake to call Mom," she whispered.

"A mistake?" I quietly inquired. I could feel her despair as she began to weep.

"Yes, a mistake. Mom got upset when I told her I'm in therapy. She said she sure hopes I'm not using you as a crutch and insisted that there's nothing wrong with me that a trip home won't cure."

While shredding her paper hanky, Jess sputtered, "So now I don't know *what* to think." She leaned back in tearful contemplation.

I asked, "What *do* you think?"

Jess sat tall, as if she were an expert in the field.

This soliloquy followed.

"Mom's scared she'll be left behind. It's hard for her to know I'm talking to you because she and I have always been so close. But I don't plan to leave Mom out! She's lonely, and I'm all she's got. She's a worrier. I know she means well, but I wish she could understand what therapy is all about. I don't come here to hurt her! I love my mom!"

I've heard clients of all ages who tenderly wish that a mother, father, partner, or friend could understand their therapeutic efforts. Harold Ross, by contrast, told me his concerns.

Harold Ross

Harold Ross, a banker, requested consultation to discuss his worries about his daughter. He proudly announced that his two sons were "Just great! Good wives, good jobs, fine homes!" It was his daughter, Rebecca, who hadn't visited or called for six months.

"What concerns me," Harold reported matter-of-factly, "is that Rebecca's been in therapy for two years—some therapist down South, you know. I'm wondering whether that therapist is putting false ideas into her head, like maybe she's trying to make her mad at me—at us—for the way we raised her."

"What kind of weird ideas do you have in mind?" I asked, with interest.

"Well, I don't know. Rebecca doesn't visit any more. Maybe she thinks she was abused or neglected or messed up in some way. Now, we're a fine family. Church every Sunday!"

Harold Ross was becoming increasingly agitated. With clenched fists he looked down—in deep thought.

"Rebecca was a sweet little girl," he reflected wistfully as his large frame relaxed. "But I got pretty rough with her. I've never told anyone this, but I think I was much too rough with Rebecca. Not her mom, me. Her mom wouldn't hurt a flea."

"So her mom was gentle and you were sometimes rough?" I clarified, while feeling deep respect for Harold's honesty.

"Yes, I was rough with Rebecca and sometimes lost control."

Harold's body began to heave wildly, like a tree fighting a hurricane.

"I feel ashamed when I remember those days," he confessed. "I was scared about my job, I drank too much, and got rough with Rebecca. I toss in bed at night and can't sleep. I ask myself, 'Did I ruin Rebecca?'"

A stout man and very tall, Harold swayed forward. He started tapping his foot frantically, then exploded into tears. He cried so hard that the leather chair shook.

"It takes courage to look back on one's life as a parent, doesn't it?" I commented quietly as his weeping subsided.

"Poor little Rebecca." Harold nodded as he regained his composure. "I feel so guilty, I don't know what to do!"

Although I, too, wasn't sure what he "should do," I suggested that before doing anything, we might meet again to think about Harold's life.

Harold left my office stating that he didn't know how to convey his love to Rebecca and he wanted to start therapy. This was the last thing he, a sixty-year-old banker, had ever considered!

During our months together, Harold reviewed his own life—including his childhood years as the son of a bitter and battering businessman. More importantly, Harold reestablished his relationship with Rebecca. He asked what was bothering her and listened intently to her anger and pain. By answering every question she asked—even when it hurt—he conveyed his love.

A man of rock-like integrity, Harold earned his daughter's profound regard as well as my own.

Rebecca now works at her father's bank while she studies to be a Certified Public Accountant.

The stories of Jessica and Harold Ross may seem like extreme examples, but they represent thousands of similar ones heard daily by clinicians around the world.

People seek therapy because of frustrations and disappointments in the arena of love. Parents seek the affection of their children. Adult children want the respect of their parents. Spouses want to understand each other. People do *not* seek therapy because they hate their parents, partners, or peers. Rather, they initiate treatment because they don't like something about themselves.

Because of the privacy inherent to individual therapy, cycles of silence perpetuate needless misunderstandings. When people begin therapy, unexpected situations can occur outside the treatment room. Clients may become pensive or preoccupied. Sometimes, in an effort to take charge of their lives, they grow distant, moody, or demanding.

Parents, partners, and peers are often curious and worried about what happens in the therapist's office and wonder what's being said about them. Many agonize, "Am I at fault?" "Will I be misrepresented?" "Did I do something wrong?"

My work with individual clients is an important basis from which the problems of this book's characters have been gleaned. In addition to talking with clients, I've interviewed parents, colleagues, and adult friends. To assure the privacy of the individuals to whom I refer, their stories have been composited. Any resemblances between actual people and individuals discussed in this book are coincidental. I'm deeply grateful to my clients for their contributions to this book.

CHAPTER 1

To The Parents and Loved Ones of People in Therapy

It is good to be merry and wise
It is good to be honest and true;
'Tis well to be off with the old love
Before you go on with the new.

Anon.

Dear Mom and Dad,

I'm writing you this letter because I miss you. I know I haven't come home for a long time, but it won't always be this way.

Years ago, although I told you that I wasn't doing well, I didn't tell you why. The fact is, I'd grown very depressed.

Since I'm not so unhappy these days, I have the energy to write. I won't say much. The reason I stayed away is that I'd gotten pretty down on myself, I couldn't sleep, and I was angry about the wrong things. I'm still that way sometimes, but not as often. I wanted you to be proud of me, but was failing miserably at everything I tried.

Last year I was having panic attacks, and I didn't want to see you at all. I was afraid I'd say things that would hurt you and embarrass myself.

I started to see a therapist two years ago. I didn't want to tell

7

you. I was afraid you'd think I was a "crazy nut," like you used to call Aunt Jane.

Well, I'm not a nut. By now I think I can lead a worthwhile life. I have a good job and nice friends, mainly artists. But I worry that you won't like me. I'm not the doctor you'd hoped I'd be. I'll never be rich. I still tend to be sloppy. Sometimes I get pretty anxious. Nevertheless, I'm beginning to like myself.

I hope, when we see each other, you'll be able to respect me for who I really am. And I want to respect you even though we've had some rough times together.

This is a hard letter to write. When I'm more sure of myself I won't be so sensitive about your opinions. At least, that's what my therapist says.

Please write. I'm sorry about anything I've ever said that hurt you. I'm trying to take charge of my life for the first time. I'm doing the best I can.

Love,
John

(John, age 28, never sent this letter to his parents.)

BE "OFF" WITH THE "OLD LOVE"?

You can discern John's effort to become his own person, separate from his parents. John's goal was to "let go" of self-criticism and self-hate. He needed an immense amount of time to nurture what was of value within himself. Interestingly, John claimed he'd been close to his parents. Although his parents had never been outwardly critical of him, John needed time to acknowledge the discrepancy between his ideal sense of who he *should* be ("just like Dad") and the person he really was. Much of John's work, as with most adults, focused on becoming his own person, psychologically separate and distinct from his parents.

Although the concept of letting go of the old to make

room for the new can be found in history, ballads, and myths, the journey of life is not, really, as the lyrics at the beginning of this chapter would suggest. For the last two lines imply that you should be "off" (finished, done) with the old before moving on with the new. In actuality, to move ahead with life, you must review, grieve, and embrace what has been. The truth is that you can never be completely done with the past.

REASONS FOR SEEKING THERAPY

Why do so many people seek therapy these days? There is one simple answer: they are all in pain. Many admit they're confused, lonely, or suffering in ways they can't explain. As with John, who wrote the letter to his parents, darkness overshadows joy. Although there may be a crisis that prompts a person's first call to the therapist's office, the true reasons adults seek treatment become clear only with time. People seek help because their lives are disappointing or out of control. They wonder why life is not turning out as they had hoped.

Quite often, new clients have already travelled many roads to diminish their discomfort. They may have read self-help books, taken extra vacations, changed jobs or relation-ships, or joined new religious groups. Frequently these solo ventures fail to reduce their suffering. At the point of total discouragement, they finally decide they can not solve their problems alone. With courage and humility, they make their first call to the therapist's office.

Clients do not seek therapy because they want to let off steam at their parents, partners, or peers. At the outset of treat-ment, most people are fiercely protective of their loved ones. Hungry for closeness, they speak lovingly of relatives. As stated by a rabbi with whom I once worked, "I always thought my mother was perfect. You'll never hear an unkind word about my mother. I'd feel disloyal if I spoke against her. But I must admit, she is very formal. When I hug her she feels like a stone statue." He paused. "Just speaking like this makes me nervous. So let's talk about me."

Clients do not enter therapy out of hatred towards their parents. If anything, they seek help because of hatred towards themselves. Their therapeutic efforts show that they are resourceful enough to take charge of their lives in disciplined ways. I have never worked with a client who, like John, didn't deeply yearn for the love of his or her parents. I have never consulted with an older adult who didn't crave affection of his or her children. The same holds true for spouses and partners.

Some years ago, I worked with Jayne, a beautiful woman who was then sixty-eight years of age. Her glowing white hair framed her face in radiance. Although she was an artist who had inspired students to create prize-winning sculptures, she sought therapy because of her feelings of loneliness and isolation. Having withdrawn from the art world which she loved, Jayne wondered whether her unhappiness had increased since her children had moved to distant states.

One day, in reviewing her years as a young widow, Jayne wept while sitting in her patterned rocker. "What was my sin?" she sobbed. "What was my sin?" She commented that her four children had required long years of therapy. One was overcoming a drinking problem. Another was struggling in her career. The youngest was gay. From miles away, Jayne attempted to claim full responsibility for their difficulties. From my vantage point, her children seemed to be proceeding courageously with their lives. Yet, Jayne insisted she had "failed" at her most important life task.

With time, Jayne learned that her depression had multiple causes. First, she had internalized too much guilt and responsibility for her adult children's problems. She gave herself no credit for raising four children *alone*. Second, she resisted establishing a new family of friends. Finally, having never mourned her husband's early death, she unknowingly converted sadness into paralyzing depression. She now had the time to acknowledge what she had lost but could never retrieve.

As Jayne's self-recrimination lessened, she began to laugh at herself. She painted in brighter colors. One day she brought me a humorous pastel sketch of herself, a woman cloaked in black who, looking in a mirror, saw herself as a dancing bride in a shining yellow gown. "Enough grief, for now!" she proclaimed.

"IT'S GOOD TO BE MERRY AND WISE"

Yes, it is good to be merry and wise. This is why I love to laugh with my patients. Adults who seek therapy are serious folk with serious issues, so they're often startled when I smile or chuckle about an unusual predicament. Delight and merriment are ways of conveying affection.

Although people start therapy for hosts of reasons, suffering is almost always related to frustrations of affection. Like Jayne, many individuals can't honor themselves for their accomplishments. Others lack the capacity to enjoy other people. As stated by Gail, an insightful young dancer, on her second day of therapy, "I want to be able to love . . . again."

I stress the universal quest for love, because it is so central to the work we therapists do. And to you who are parents, partners, and peers of people in therapy, I will emphasize this crucial quest over and over again.

THERAPY: THE MYSTERY, MYSTIQUE, AND MISCONCEPTION

Many who read this book have completed successful therapy journeys. For you, the "mystique" of the therapist's office doesn't exist. If your therapist was skilled and empathetic, you may recall your treatment hours as valuable times of self-healing.

But for those of you who have coped with life's challenges through other means, therapy often remains a mystery. One mature woman, a good friend of mine, is puzzled by the work I do. From time to time she looks at me quizzically and asks, "Now, what, again, do you do with those people?" Some view therapists simply as listeners who offer encouragement or kindly advice. Others nervously recall personal experiences with ineffective or unethical clinicians. Cartoons and sit-coms suggest that therapists bungle through life as much as everybody else. Perhaps they're right. In any case, you deserve to know how therapy works.

When parents learn that their adult children have started psychotherapy, they invariably wonder "why?" A range of other questions, fantasies, and feelings soon flood their minds. On the following pages, I'll discuss some of the reasons people seek treatment, as well as various reactions which you—as loved ones—can expect. I will also deal with situations that typically arise, and a few of the outcomes you might anticipate. I have addressed specific chapters to partners, friends, siblings, and employers because some of their questions differ from those of parents. The entire book, however, will help all of you to understand the therapy process and its impact on family and friendship networks.

The loved ones and parents of people in therapy are my first concern: as the loved ones of those clients of whom I write you have shared significant moments and feelings in their lives. As parents, you raised these people who now share their narratives with us. Because of your early bonding with them and their primary attachments to you, they can form meaningful alliances with others.

Parents and loved ones need reassurance that these therapists are ethical and well-trained. How seriously do clinicians reflect upon the plights of young people? How responsible are therapists, really?

Tammy and Helen, Her Mother

When I was much younger and had just begun my practice, I wandered on a Sunday afternoon through our local art museum. Tammy, a lovely girl of eighteen who was my client, came rushing towards me across the gallery floor. Flushed and breathless, she exclaimed, "My mother is with me! Come! You simply must meet my mother!" She ran back across the gallery, grasped her mother's hand, and dragged her to the statue where I stood. I smiled at this attractive matriarch. We shook hands warmly and commented briefly about the displays. However, as Tammy and her mother bade me farewell, I wondered how this mature woman, whose life experience was far greater than mine, felt about my sharing her daughter's secrets.

It is rare that we clinicians have the opportunity to meet the parents of our clients. I, like Tammy, enjoyed the "joining together" of these "mysterious worlds." Most of all, I felt the depth of my responsibility to both Helen and her daughter who was now, at least temporarily, in my care.

As therapists, we assume responsibility for our clients but only briefly. It is we, not you, who will ultimately say "farewell" to those we treat.

I doubt I will ever meet Helen again, but our meeting in the museum highlights the necessary ethical boundary which typically emerges between parents and their adult children's therapists. Perhaps some of the discomfort felt by parents is the result of this required distance between themselves and the people their children have sought out for help.

Frank Jones and His Son

Several years ago, Frank Jones, a balding sixty-five-year-old widower, was referred to me by the therapist of his son. Frank, a businessman and devotee of fly fishing, stated that he had been completely "thrown" by the fact that *his* son—a lawyer—would need therapy. Frank spoke angrily of his belief that problems should be kept in the family, and asked if I knew anything about "this Dr. Z" who was treating his son Jim?

I responded to his barrage of questions by commenting, "You have strong feelings, don't you, about your son's therapy?"

"Indeed I *do*!" Frank almost shouted. "I was a good father, and his mother, when alive, couldn't have loved Jim more. We were an active family. It was always 'family first!' I can assure you that Jim came from a happy home."

"Did anyone ever say that he did *not* come from a caring home and that you were *not* a caring father?" I quietly inquired.

"Well, I don't like to think that he's talking behind my back."

Once again I asked, "Did anyone ever imply that you were *not* a caring dad?"

At this point Frank choked up. He grabbed an unironed handkerchief from his suit pocket.

"No, not really. But during my war years, I worried about my wife and the kids. When I came home, I was irritable and distracted. I was not the father I wanted to be. I wasn't close to my dad, so I'd hoped I could be a real dad to Jim."

"And did anyone ever say that you weren't a 'real dad' to Jim?"

Frank looked up, startled.

"Well no, not really. Actually, no." He looked down again, thinking. "Perhaps I'm the only one who has wondered this. I've asked myself many times whether I was a good dad.

While I'm fishing, I wish Jim were by the stream with me. I wonder if I failed him. I worry that I didn't take him fishing more often. He's never said I failed. I'm my own best critic. I always was."

As Frank prepared to leave the office, he looked at me with an embarrassed smile. "You know," he said, "I think I'm jealous of his therapist. He'll get to know Jim better than I do."

"Only for a brief time," I responded. "You will always be Jim's dad."

Parents and loved ones respond in different ways to the news that their child or companion is unhappy and seeking therapy. Some express relief, if not joy—"Things will get better for Mary!" Others claim that they wouldn't seek therapy for themselves, but they're glad their children are giving thought to their lives. Other parents and loved ones grieve, as did Mr. Jones, feeling guilty and dismissed. Many fear that they will be blamed for the other person's unhappiness. Unclear about the underlying dynamics of the therapeutic process, some openly oppose therapy. They may attack the person or the therapist feeling that therapy will damage their companion or offspring, lead them astray, misguide them spiritually—or worse—alienate them.

In most cases, parents feel sad that their adult children are turning to others for understanding. This parental melancholy is both understandable and painfully familiar. We invest the major portion of our lives into raising these fine folk who then go off to admire and confide in someone else!

For parents like Jayne or Frank, a process of "self review" is automatically triggered when children start therapy. "What did I do wrong?" "What will be said about me?" "Have I failed my children?" "Oh, God, forgive me for those angry words!"

I hope that as you read these pages, you will become less threatened by your child's therapy. I will urge you to honor yourself as the figure who nurtured your young until they grew old enough to grapple with their own lives.

THE HARD FACTS

People enter therapy for lots of reasons. Some adults want to discuss self-esteem, work, and relationships with someone outside the family. Other issues, such as sexual dysfunction, are difficult to discuss with parents, loved ones, or friends. Many personal problems relate more to constitution, genetic predisposition, and peer pressure than to family upbringing. One hard fact is that none of us are perfect as parents, loved ones, or friends. Another hard fact is that who you are, with all your blemishes, may indeed be a part of the other person's therapy discourse.

If you are a parent, loved one, or friend, can you accept the reality that, despite your own difficult childhood and all your loving effort, you probably *did* make your share of parenting or relationship "mistakes?" If you are relaxed about your own vulnerabilities, the other person will feel freer to tell you about his or hers.

Successful therapy demands that clients acknowledge "the truth." Some truths are emotional truths: the truth about what one really feels and thinks. Buried feelings and reawakened memories invite shocking surprises. Many people fiercely maintain age-old myths about themselves, others, the past, and the future. These frustrated adults slide into unhappy predicaments and cannot move forward.

While your children, partners, and peers in therapy retrieve and enhance themselves in honest ways, you can help by facing the truths of your own life. By relinquishing the impossible fantasy that you were "parent-perfect," "friend-perfect," or "partner-perfect," you will set the stage for happier relationships.

CHAPTER 2

"Now What, Again, is 'Therapy'?"

Each Thanksgiving, Anna sits at the dinner table. She admires her grandchildren, the centerpiece, and golden turkey. With time, and as conversation increases to its annual pitch, she turns to her son—a well-known psychiatrist—and asks, "Now tell me again, Les; what is it you *do* with these patients you see?"

Each year as her son, Doctor Les Jackson, scoops stuffing from the bird onto the platter, he simply responds, "We just talk."

"Just talk?" mutters Anna. "I've been talking to people for years."

Anna's confusion about the work of a therapist is founded in the past. She was raised on the flatlands of Indiana where farming families worked together, prayed together, and sang together. She fed dozens of farmhands around her large oak table. She sewed her own bridal gown. There was always work to do and everyone pitched in. Long hours were spent tilling fields or preparing jams. "When *we* had problems," she murmured to herself, "we just solved them."

Times were different in Anna's youth. This is not to say that problems were never solved. There were, however, fewer choices, less over-stimulation, and generally, intact family groups. Whether grandmother "really" loved grandfather was simply not discussed. Children were strictly disciplined and sometimes abused. Many children died young, filling cemeteries with tiny tombstones. But people, both rich and poor, persevered with the work of survival. In the past, far less was known about unnecessary psychic pain.

"So what is it, again, that you *do* with these patients?" asks Les's mother each year.

Feeling annoyed and unappreciated, Les Jackson responds again, "We just talk."

"Oh," says his mother, looking at her plate. Anna is much too intelligent to feel satisfied with his lazy response.

Mental health professionals are partially responsible for the misunderstandings between those who understand what therapy is and those who do not. Freud's pioneering explorations into the unconscious processes led to a new form of non-medical psychiatry. His work was coined "the talking cure."

"But what do you talk *about*?" persists Anna.

Les, serving a second portion of turkey to his daughter, simply answers, "Problems."

"Well," Anna grumbles to herself, "I've been talking with people about *problems* for eighty-four years."

TYPES OF THERAPY

Theories of Mental Health and Mental Suffering

All legitimate schools of psychiatry, clinical social work, psychology, and other mental health disciplines require that students study the theories—or basic principles—of mental functioning. Students review the issues of infant and adolescent development, and continue up through the psychological tasks of adult life.

For example, recent infant research allows us to predict the essential developmental tasks of the child (such as crawling away from its mom and shuffling right back) as it proceeds through each month of early life. Mastery of each task prepares the child for its next challenge. There are many studies which illuminate the critical milestones of human development from infancy through old age. Research findings assist clinicians because they help to explain why so many people fail to master the healthy development tasks.

Some individuals are highly sophisticated in terms of intellect but are nonetheless sad and emotionally dreary. Others are so chronically overwhelmed with intense emotions that they can't concentrate on mental pursuits. Seemingly charming men and women may own enviable social skills, but in intimate relationships they may grow aloof, shy, or assaultive. These contradictions indicate that, human differences aside, their key developmental tasks may have been blocked at specific phases of development. Such contradictions are the cues which mental health workers note in assessing the underlying aspects of a client's unique problems.

There are other roadblocks. What happens to the mind and emotions of a child who is physically abused or overlooked because she is so "sweet and good?" How does the little girl explain to herself that, after the birth of her brother, she is no longer "Daddy's little princess?" What transpires in the mind of a child who's left alone too much, or loses a parent, or moves too often from school to school? How do children explain to themselves the angry fights between parents, or more mysteriously, their parents' polite, but hostile interactions?

The child must make some kind of sense of its world if he or she is to continue developing socially, intellectually, and spiritually. So what mechanisms are used, within the child's mind, to explain contradictory parental messages? A mother is red with rage but proclaims she's relaxed. A child feels sad but is told to smile. These types of directives and "mislabels" confound the young mind that is determined to make sense of the only world it knows.

Some adults, raised by trustworthy parents, see only the good in others. Therefore, they conclude that the world is a safer place than, in some settings, it actually is. Others, raised in violent neighborhoods or abusive homes, conclude that no one can ever be trusted. Because the developing mind seeks clarity, many youthful conclusions are ill-founded.

Janice, a woman of twenty-five, was reared in the religious home of an ambassador. She sought help for transitory depression after her dashing boyfriend physically assaulted her. One day, still bruised from the attack, Janice tilted her dark hair to the side. In deep thought, she looked up and said:

"My problem is that I trust too much. I expect people to be reasonable and honest. I assume that each guy will be as dignified as Dad. It's terrible to lose your faith in the 'good.' But some people are absolutely cruel."

Janice wept quietly. She spoke of the good times she'd had as a child, while knowing that a return to childhood's safety was impossible.

We are constantly reorganizing information about ourselves and the people around us. If your boss looks at you angrily, you try to make sense of it. You may think, "She's in a bad mood today!" Or you may shrink away in fear, predicting: "I'm about to be fired." All of us, without knowing it, are constantly assessing the incoming data that surrounds us.

The experiences we have growing up with our families, as well as our on-going life events, determine our ways of coping with the world. The coping skills that children develop to survive are typically creative and deeply implanted in their unconscious minds. Long-standing assumptions about the most predictable outcomes for our actions influence the basic choices we make. Some people's conclusions accurately match the realities of who they are and the best ways to proceed with their lives. For other people, assumptions about the way things will turn out rarely mirror the realities of daily living. Most people who enter into therapy have suddenly realized that their original tools for survival simply aren't working any more.

I'm reminded of the young dancer, Zoe, who told me during her second consultation that she wanted to "be able to love . . . again." Because of the childhood death of a cherished brother, she'd grown frozen to intimate loving. Happily, somewhere in her unconscious reservoir, she knew what it felt like to love. Because of Zoe's early life crisis, she'd concluded on an unconscious level that "if you love, you lose." Unfortunately, she'd been quarreling with her big brother when he died. Therefore, she'd decided that "if you get angry, you kill." In addition, since her brother died during an epileptic fit, she'd decided that "when people get excited, they die." Furthermore, Zoe was convinced that the best way to deal with sadness was to "cheer people up." After all, that's how she'd tried to reclaim her grieving parents' attention.

At age six, Zoe had been too young to verbalize her faulty reasoning. Furthermore, her conclusions were formed on an unconscious level. This is why, despite all her efforts to fall in love, she could not succeed. During her therapeutic journey, Zoe was able to retrieve forgotten memories of her brother's death. With the help of her therapist, she could finally grieve over her losses and revise her conclusions about the dangers of affection. Joyously relieved, she eventually found that she could freely love again. Her wedding invitation was signed with flowers and flair.

Some individuals slip rather easily into psychotic mental states whereas others can't even recall their nightly dreams. Despite high moral standards, good citizens may find themselves lying to colleagues, engaging in sexual affairs, assaulting loved ones, or pilfering screwdrivers at the local hardware store. They then arrive in the therapist's office baffled and afraid.

It's the clinician's job to understand the roots of a wide range of conflicts so that the most essential issues can be targeted during the treatment hour. If the professional has not studied the unconscious mechanisms of symptom formation, a lot of time may be wasted with "just talk."

This is not to say that psychotherapists don't just talk with their clients. Many people seek consultation regarding parenting concerns, transitional adjustments, vocational questions, and other issues. These requests invite focused, brief discussions about current decisions. Not all clients are symptomatic. However, a qualified professional must be prepared to work with a wide range of issues—from the more simple uncertainties of everyday life to the profoundly pathological.

Some psychological theories focus rigorously on intellectual or cognitive processes. Others focus on human behavior. Important research has unlocked genetic truths about severe mental illness. There are many schools of psychology and each offers new knowledge to the field. All theory bases share one common factor: an interest in mental and emotional processes. The theory base of your loved one's psychotherapist forms his or her context for dealing with their concerns. It will also affect the way in which the therapist decides to work with your child or partner. However, the theoretical framework of a clinician is only one aspect of successful psychotherapy. This brings us to the question of "technique."

Techniques and the Art of Patient Care

Just as therapists approach client care from different theory bases, they also interact with their clients in contrasting ways. These variations will influence changes you'll observe in your loved ones while they are in therapy.

Because clinicians' styles differ, your own experiences if you were ever in therapy may be vastly different from those of your child or partner. Equally different might have been "Aunt Jane's" therapy which, as reported by her nephew, "didn't help a bit."

In addition, the same clinician may intentionally choose to work differently with different people. In working with a potentially psychotic client, the therapist may be gentle and directive while focusing on such basic tasks of living as how to use public transportation or regulate medications. The same clinician, with a depressed older woman, may be quiet and receptive while attempting to enter her client's emotional world. With a shy teenager, however, this therapist may become lively and animated. With a professional liar, the clinician may be dynamically confrontational.

Some therapists choose to do short-term, goal-oriented work. Others recommend group, family, or couples therapy. Yet many therapists prefer working with individuals in an unhurried, unstructured way. This approach allows new insights and feelings to arise at the client's natural pace.

Perhaps most important to parents of people in therapy is the awareness that many therapists openly encourage their clients to directly confront their parents about "damages" these children feel their parents have caused them. Although this is not the way I choose to work, it is a common technique.

The Directive Therapist Who Recommends Confrontations

A book which you may have seen in store windows by Susan Forward, Ph.D., is titled *Toxic Parents*. The author recommends "short-term therapy that focuses on changing destructive behavior patterns." The book instructs the client to "calmly but firmly tell . . . parents about the negative events that he or she remembers from . . . childhood."

Forward states that the purpose of the confrontation is to "face up to them, to overcome once and for all your fear of facing up to them, to tell your parents the truth, and to determine the type of relationship you can have with them from now on."

If your child is working with a clinician who is directive, you can anticipate being confronted openly and firmly, presumably for the sake of your son's or daughter's emotional well-being.

Many clinicians give direct advice, follow a systematic plan, and believe that the client's return to the parent for a direct confrontation may help to heal the inner child. Forward suggests that "people can forgive toxic parents, but they should do it at the conclusion—not at the beginning—of their emotional housecleaning."

The Non-Directive Therapist Who Focuses on Internal Struggles

Some clinicians would disagree with Forward's assertion that therapeutic trends have moved away from exploring the relationships between past and current emotional patterns. Insight-oriented therapists might argue that although a client can learn to "stand up" to the parent, the actual confrontation would not promote lasting changes within the conscious and unconscious world of the client.

I am reminded of a preliminary lecture once offered by a psychoanalytically-oriented psychiatrist to a group of experienced clinicians. He was lecturing on techniques for conducting the initial interview with a client. Morris Dow stated, "In conducting the initial interview, and throughout the patient's treatment, we want to help the patient to see that his or her problems are *internal* . . . that the struggle, now, is within the patient. Therefore, we must help the patient to define the struggle as his or her own. Help him to take responsibility for the struggle . . . instead of focusing on a 'bad parent' or a 'bad family.'"

Many theorists are guarded about dramatizing or searching for parental deficits. By observing and discussing a client's dreams, patterns of behavior and mood, fantasies, and false assumptions, non-directive therapists focus on internal struggles. Although seriously injured adults may feel compelled to challenge parents about past (and present) violations of their integrity, insight-oriented therapists rarely recommend these confrontations. They insist that the client's conflicts are now his or her own. Furthermore, say the non-directive therapists, frustrations from the past which plague adult clients reflect only "aspects," or parts, of early parenting figures and experiences. Beatrice, a twenty-six-year-old preschool teacher exemplifies this theory.

Beatrice

One sunny morning, Bea sat down and looked at me. "So last week you said that the war is more inside than outside of me. Now, what did you mean?"

"What comes to mind?" I responded, assuming she had already given thought to my comment.

"Well, for some reason, I kept thinking how guilty I feel about being impolite. It's as if I carry all these tapes in my head that say: '*guilty, guilty, guilty.*' I was really watching myself this week because you said, 'The war's within yourself.'"

Beatrice proceeded to tell the following story:

"On Saturday, I went to pick up my photographs. I was excited because they included by graduation pictures. I'd waited in line for twenty minutes, so I wasn't in a good mood when I finally got to the cashier. Then, when he handed me my photos, I noticed that they were in black and white instead of color. I was very angry because I'd waited a month to have the pictures. I was counting on showing them to my boyfriend while he was in town. So I said to the salesman, 'I wanted the photos in color.'

"'But, miss,' he said, 'look here. You put a mark next to black and white.' I looked at the envelope, and sure enough, it said 'black and white.'"

"Well, you couldn't pay me to have black and white graduation pictures. I knew someone had made a mistake.

"So I said, 'Excuse me, sir, but I didn't write this here. You'll have to do the job again.' I could feel myself getting hot.

"At this point the salesman said, 'Well, you'll have to pay for both sets.'

"Over my dead body, I thought to myself. And that's when I heard this tape in my head. It was my mother's voice, saying, 'Beatrice, I raised you to be a *lady*.'

"The manager came out and I almost screamed, 'I ordered my photos in color, and these are in black and white!' I was fuming and I'm sure he could tell.

"'But, miss,' he said, 'these are expensive photographs. We'll replace them, but you'll have to pay for both sets.'

"By then I was in a rage. I asked to see the file they keep in the back of the shop where they do the work. Sure enough, there was the envelope *I'd* filled out—with *color* marked clearly by my signature.

"I was relieved, but almost in tears because I was so mad.

"'So now!' I almost yelled at the manager, 'I expect you to remake these photos and I must have them by this Monday!.'

"The manager looked ruffled, and I know I wasn't acting ladylike.

"I left the store, and all I could hear was my mother's voice: 'Bea, you must always be a lady. You must forgive. You must be kind—at all times.'

"I felt like a dog who stole food from the kitchen table and walked away with her tail between her legs. If my mother had seen how angry I'd been, she would have died. In fact, it was as if my mother had been in the shop and seen the whole thing.

"So I think this was my internal war.

"On the one hand, I told myself, 'Bea, you had a right to be angry and upset.'

"But on the other hand, I kept hearing Mother's voice say, 'Bea, you must act like a lady: forgiving and kind.'

"It was as if Mom was both inside of me, talking, and outside of me, watching. At the same time I was inside of me, talking, and outside of me, watching.

"This is *my* internal struggle."

Many insight-oriented clinicians prefer to have clients explore their emotions in the therapist's office. This way, anger, grief, and memories can be explored with high degrees of understanding. Non-directive clinicians tend to be more quiet, because they know that the misunderstandings occurring between them and their clients will reflect important information about the client's internal conflicts.

A psychodynamically-oriented clinician would thus be less inclined to "direct" a client's actions (such as confronting one's parents) outside of the therapy office. With time, this type of therapeutic relationship allows clients to revise faulty assumptions about themselves, their relationships, and the broader world. Although these therapists may give occasional advice, the client's job is to understand the contradictions within him or herself.

This non-directive therapeutic style does tend to take longer and will probably cost more money. But many believe that long-lasting changes can only occur with more intensive psychotherapy which focuses on deeply internalized conflicts and sorrow. As one client put it, "It took me twenty-five years to get this mixed up; I guess I'll need at least two years to get fixed." Insight-oriented clinicians recommend either open-ended or short-term treatment plans. These determinations are based on the client's needs and capacity for insight, financial resources, and stated objectives.

There are many other techniques for therapy. Each technical approach offers a special focus and method for helping adults (as individuals, couples, or entire families) to live more gratifying lives.

As the parents and loved ones of people in therapy, you should keep in mind that theoretical and technical styles vary. If your adult child or partner works with a directive clinician, you should respond constructively to painfully earnest confrontations. Be prepared to handle these challenges in ways that inspire mutual growth and greater understanding.

On the other hand, if your loved one is working with a non-directive clinician who focuses primarily on internal conflicts, you may notice on-going signs of your loved one's evolving identity. There are other things which might influence and color the success of your loved one's therapy.

I will discuss the way theoretical positions and technical styles vary, as do the outcomes of these diverse forms of therapy.

The Therapist's Personality and Philosophical Base: The Therapeutic Fit

If you are considering therapy for yourself or are helping a loved one locate a clinician, you may want to read more about contrasting types of psychotherapy. You'll also want to inquire about the technical style of a prospective clinician. However, in selecting a therapist, one variable remains elusive: the personality of the therapist.

Although some professionals would disagree, I believe that the basic "fit" between client and therapist is a critical factor in treatment that should not be overlooked. Most well-trained professionals can do adequate work with those who are entrusted to them. However, in consulting with client groups, I've found that the temperament, disposition, and even philosophical outlook of the therapist profoundly influence the treatment process. For this reason, professionals recommend that people interview several clinicians before committing themselves to therapy. Choosing a therapist from the phone book or a newspaper ad is riskier than obtaining names from respected friends.

Many outstanding psychotherapists, in conducting a first interview, will seem reserved, neutral, and quiet. They are setting the stage for a human drama which focuses on the client—not the therapist. Other gifted clinicians relate spontaneously and engagingly. They ask questions and display emotion.

Indeed, their personalities differ. However, having interviewed two therapists with similar training, a prospective client may feel a special compatibility with one consultant and not with the other. He or she may have sensed the clinician's energy, interest, or passion for the work. In contrast, the client may feel emotionally calmed, soothed, or eager to work. The prospective client is the best judge of which clinician provides a good "fit."

Whether this special fit is based on the clinician's temperament, personality, or an elusive "something else," clients should leave consultations feeling understood and more hopeful. These are cues that an essential connection has been made, that the clinician has grasped an important message.

Do not underestimate the importance of the relationship that will ensue between therapist and client. Good psychotherapy demands far more than theory and technique. Truly gifted clinicians are artists. While working with them, the client becomes creative. Together, they attend to the client's art of living.

"I Know It's Not My Business, but . . ."

Several years ago, I received a call from the mother of a thirty-three-year-old woman with whom I had met only four times.

"I know it's not my business," said the mother hesitantly over the phone, "but I wondered how Sally is doing."

I explained to Mrs. Murphy that I cannot talk on the phone about anyone without obtaining permission first. I tried to convey to Mrs. Murphy that I was sure her call was well-intentioned.

But Mrs. Murphy persisted, saying, "Well, I know it's not my business, but . . . did you know that Sally's about to lose her job and rarely calls me anymore?"

Again, I responded that if Mrs. Murphy had concerns about someone I work with, she should speak directly to that person. I repeated that surely her call was well-intentioned.

"I guess it's not my business," said Sally's mother sadly as we said goodbye.

I do not like to be evasive. However, a cardinal rule of psychotherapy is confidentiality. If a client feels the therapist is talking behind his or her back, the therapy will not survive.

Indeed, Mrs. Murphy's relationship with Sally is very much her business. I did not mean to be rude, but Sally's work in here is *her* business. As her mother, Mrs. Murphy must discuss her concerns with Sally herself.

By now you may be wondering, "How much more do I really need to know if my child's therapy is not my business?" The answer, of course, is "absolutely nothing."

However, calls from parents like Mrs. Murphy remind me that many parents and partners are curious and concerned about what their loved ones are doing in therapy. These people want their spouses and offspring to be happy, but also wonder whether they are still loved.

For example, if you're the parent of an adult child in therapy, no matter how close or far away that child lives, the psychological changes in both you and your offspring will intertwine in subtle, if not obvious, ways. You may note that your son or daughter calls you less frequently, or you may receive challenging letters and questions. Similarly, transitions in your own life may deeply affect your children. If you're now engrossed in new activities or have remarried, your adult kids may wonder whether you're glad they're out of the house. I'm often impressed by the strong reactions of young adults when they return home only to find that their bedrooms have been converted into studies or guest rooms!

Beth

"Mom's only failing is that she treats me like a child!" fumed Beth, a twenty-eight year old math teacher. "Mom constantly worries and asks about my therapy and did I tell my therapist that it's all Dad's fault? And am I aware of the dangers in the world? And did I buy a proper suit for the interview? I adore my mom but she drives me nuts! I tell her to get off my back! Others think I'm competent. Why can't Mom?"

If you're a parent, you naturally feel hurt by protests like Beth's. After all, you're only trying to help. Would her anger feel less insulting if you could speak with her therapist? The answer is unclear. But given the choice, Beth just might not invite you in.

Although you and your adult children may be moving on with your distinctly separate lives, families are still families. It's your choice whether you want to make your son's or daughter's business your business. If your son or daughter is in therapy, surprising changes can ripple through the entire family whether you decide to get involved or not. Prepare yourself for revisions of the family norm. If you educate yourself about the therapy process, you may find it easier to respect your child's choices. Your child needs your respect. In fact, it may be on the top of his or her wish list.

The Ripple Effect

I believe in the "ripple effect." Within any group, if one person changes, others are affected. In any system or organization of individuals, a small change in one place brings about a small change in others. Sometimes, like a row of dominoes, a simple tap on one end sends every one toppling.

Last summer, while fishing off a pier to which people had travelled hundreds of miles, no one caught a single fish. Seventy-five of us had packed the pier, since word had gone out that this would be a "good" day. Hours rolled by, children became restless, the bait grew warm. Parents carried small infants back to their trucks to nap. The sun was hot. But no one went home. The pier stretched far, far out to sea. A lazy, quiet day.

Late that afternoon, a sleepy old man with a pipe and red hat stood up straight. He quietly pulled from the blue-green water not one flounder but three! He was quiet, graceful, and private about his prizes.

Not a word was spoken. But through the "ripple effect," the good news spread down the pier within seconds. Children stopped whining. Women returned from the trucks. Reels started whirring. Poles shot like pistols out to sea. Within an hour, more trucks had arrived at our pier. The word was out. Fish were biting.

News travels fast through families, too. A change in one person effects changes in others. Therapists call this the ripple effect. So be advised. When you least expect it, you may suddenly awaken to the noise of your adult child's or partner's therapy journey. Even if you hadn't planned to make it "your business."

CHAPTER 3

THE FACE OF REFLECTION AND EMOTIONAL TRUTHS

It is midnight.

Carolyn and Mark Jasper, both in their mid-fifties, work hard, and are tired after a long day. Carolyn, a lively interior designer, has taken on a new client who wants her office remodeled "within a month!" Mark, a criminal lawyer, is arguing an important case tomorrow.

Collapsing into the unmade four-poster bed, they set the alarm for six o'clock.

"So how do you think Tim's doing?" asks Carolyn.

"Let's not talk about problems," mumbles Mark, rolling to the side.

"But I'm worried about Tim. He's been back for a year, and has become so silent."

"He's going to be okay," yawns Mark.

"I wish I knew what he's thinking. He never talks to us."

"He's in good hands, Carolyn, and he's a good kid," mutters Mark of his twenty-five-year-old son who returned home after a disappointing love affair.

"But, Mark, he's still not dating. He's lethargic. I just wish I knew what he's thinking."

"He'll be all right," mumbles Mark.

"Well, it's hard to live in a house with a stranger," protests Carolyn as Mark drifts off to sleep.

"Are you awake?" whispers Carolyn.

No response.

Carolyn is right. It's hard to share a home with an adult child who hardly talks. But Mark is also right: Tim will be "okay." Having found the challenges of supporting himself and coping with loneliness too severe, Tim awkwardly returned to his parents' home a year ago.

Tim feels embarrassed about his reentry into the family nest. While maintaining his distance as meticulously as possible, he's found a job at the local hardware store. Having been in therapy for eight months, he's considering one more try at community college. Some of his personal belongings are housed in a rented storage space as a sign to himself that he's "half-way out the door." Tim is easy to live with because he's tidy and respectful of the family rules. Nevertheless, he feels like a stranger in his own home. And everyone, in quiet ways, is affected by his silent presence.

The next day, Tim ambles into his therapist's office as punctually as always. At age twenty-five, he smiles the boyish grin of a fifteen-year-old. He starts talking before sheepishly sinking into the leather chair.

"I've done a lot of thinking this week, especially while fixing Dad's car. I've decided that as the youngest kid and the *misfit*, I always just followed along.

"I've always been a follower, I think. Now that I'm trying to make something of myself, I've got to admit that over the last ten years I've been waiting for someone to take me somewhere. It's kind of like you said last week: I've been sort of waiting for someone to lead me.

"So this is what I was thinking while fixing Dad's car. I've decided that I've got to take myself places.

"Right now, I'm just starting to lead myself. I'm starting really slow, like I saw Dad's car was leaking oil and I said, 'Hey, Pop! Want me to take a look?' It was my idea, you see.

"And I also decided, while fixing the car, that I don't want to go into law—absolutely not. I didn't discuss it with anyone, you see. I just decided: I don't like lawyers; I like mechanics!

"I kept on thinking, I've got no training in directing myself. No one ever asked my opinions or showed me the respect they showed my brothers. Now, I might be remembering it wrong, but that's what I feel. I just followed along, which meant, I followed just about anyone.

"Now, I decided there are lots of people you can follow. But some of the guys I followed led me wrong, like into fights and drugs.

"Some people are real leaders, but none of them have taken much interest in me. So I think it's best to be my own leader.

"So that's what I decided while I was fixing Dad's car."

Tim smiled shyly. He was pleased with himself.

His mother and father try to respect Tim's privacy. Tim tries to respect theirs. He is reflecting on problems and plans. He is quiet. His mother and father wish Tim were leading a more active life. So does Tim.

Meanwhile, Tim's stillness is active. Although he appears to be distant and removed, Tim is in deep thought. His silence is productive. He's trying to make sense of his life and where he's been. He wears the "face of reflection."

EMOTIONAL SEPARATENESS

Your adult child in therapy may not be living at home, as Carolyn and Mark's son was. Nevertheless, you may still be aware of the mental distancing that's occurring within your son or daughter. "What are our children thinking?" is a question commonly asked by parents. Knowing they shouldn't interfere too much, parents often tiptoe around their adult children. But because they're concerned, parents wonder, "What are they thinking?"

Parents of adult children are diligent. However, their children don't understand that their folks are trying as they always did to do things *right*. The tasks of maturing parents in relationship to their offspring are complex. For some parents, becoming active and nonparenting persons is a hard journey.While their kids are carving out their destinies, parents are trying to gain a glimpse of their own. For parents whose lives have been devoted to their children, an empty house echoes with memories of times past. There's no going back. In some ways, the tasks of aging parents are more unnerving than those of their children. Seeking love, they are hurt by their children's disapproving glances or absences. Adult children can still turn to their parents whether they like them or not. Parents, by contrast, must take care of themselves. Whereas parents are facing the last decades of their lives, young adults see their lives as infinite or, at least, as undefined. Young adults are still attempting to define their personal identities.

In their book *The Boomerang Kids*, Jean Okimoto and Phyllis Stegall discuss the special challenges that young adults and their parents are facing today. This practical guide, along with Monica O'Kane's *Hey, Mom, I'm Home Again!* assists parents whose children have returned to live with them. Parents like Mr. and Mrs. Jasper whisper in bed and tiptoe delicately in an effort to protect their children from their personal worries and midlife "growing pains." In the meantime, their adult children return from various forays into the world. Unable to articulate their many discomforts, young people are forced to define their separate identities. "But of course Tim is his own man!"

declares Mr. Jasper. Yet Tim, their youngest and most sensitive "child," is not so sure.

Okimoto and Stegall state, that claiming identity involves understanding that you are separate and different from your parents, even when you end up choosing to keep for yourself some of the ideas, values, or aspects of the life style with which you were raised. The most important questions to be answered are:

> *Who am I?* (not *Who do my parents want me to be?*)
> *What do I want out of life?*
> *What do I think?*
> *What is important to me?*
> *How do I want to spend my time?*
> *What kind of job do I want?*
> *What kind of people do I like?*
> *What kind of person will I love?*

We'll return to the issue of "separateness" in the next chapter since it is such a major theme for adults of all ages. Frequent shifts between intimacy and autonomy begin in infancy and repeat themselves throughout life: they are not unique to the young adult. Nor are excursions into separate, self-reflective spaces always solo acts. Separateness is always achieved while in relationships with others. "Separateness" does not mean abandonment! It's a term that defines the process of becoming aware of individuality while in relationships (either geographically or internally) with parents, partners, and peers.

Toddlers scoot away from their parents, only to return within moments. The peek-a-boo game, enjoyed by both babies and parents, is exciting because of the tense juxtaposition between being alone and then rediscovered. The same is true for hide-and-seek. "I need time alone!" weeps a midlife mother.

Yet, after her adult children have raced off to the beach, this same mother confesses, "I need people in my life!"

Key phases of development facilitate *differentiation*, the process of becoming a distinct, capable, and independent individual. The theme of *individuation* is alive and well in us all. Individuation refers to the individual's capacity to feel whole, solidly centered, and unique as an individual while in relationship to others. Two fully individuated adults may be mutually reliant on each other for love and practical assistance. The capacity for *separateness* requires that the individual, while geographically or psychologically separate from his or her partner, can cope alone with life's tasks when necessary or desired.

Why do exhausted parents weep when their children graduate from high school, depart for the military, or get married? Why do divorced people, despite horrendous marriages, continue to wonder whether they've made a mistake in leaving their mates? Why do competent individuals fall apart after the death of a spouse? At times like these, people are faced with their need for companionship. Adults on the dark hills of night gaze admiringly at the stars awed by the expansive and terrifying reality that as small humans on this earth they are, ultimately, alone.

Thus the theme of embracing oneself as unique but amazingly finite works its way through history and the stories of people's private lives. For this reason, you can surely relate to the special struggles of vulnerable people who have problems becoming psychologically separate. Although feeling self-directed may not have posed serious problems for you, you cannot assume the same is true for your partner, son, or daughter. Another's struggle may be intensely precarious.

The therapist of today is in a privileged position. Whereas the internal processes of becoming psychologically separate from one's parents are often hidden from the original family, the therapist is allowed a window into them.

Since so many parents and partners are wondering what their loved ones are thinking, I'll share with you a few insights. By joining me in the consultation room, you'll find the inner worlds of loved ones are not as mysterious as they appear.

In order to know what you want from life, you must know, quite specifically, what you think and feel. Feelings and thoughts are closely interwoven and are often difficult to differentiate. Feelings can be complex: you may both love and feel irritated toward the same person. You can feel determined and discouraged at the same time. But if a person doesn't know what he or she really thinks and feels about a person, situation, or idea, gullibility and confusion pose serious threats to integrity and safety.

EMOTIONAL TRUTHS

Contradictory emotional truths are great sources of turmoil between parents and adult children in therapy. Whereas a parent may recall his or her children's childhoods as happy if not idyllic, the children may not own the same recollections. While reviewing a specific phase of one's childhood, people in therapy may be temporarily overwhelmed with unfamiliar feelings and moods.

For example, Sue is reviewing the sadness and fear she felt when she moved to a new school in fourth grade. She had lost close friends and her favorite teacher. She was treated as the scapegoat by a group of rich kids on the new playground. As an adult, she's become stuck on a similar issue. Recently promoted, she needs to move to Arizona but feels terrified for reasons she can't understand. She simply states, "I will not move." In wondering whether she might be re-experiencing her fourth-grade trauma, Sue describes her painful grade school memories to her mother who says: "But, Sue, you were such a good traveler. You'll be happy in Arizona just as you were happy in fourth grade! You loved your new school!"

Sue now decides never to confide in her mother again. Sue is learning that she was not always as happy, successful, and adaptable as her mother routinely told Sue she was. By now she has lost the courage to reveal anything about her fears. After all, her mother would deny or dismiss her emotional realities: "But Sue! You're such a good traveler!" Because Sue loves her mother and doesn't want to hurt her, she retreats into her tortoise-like shell.

"Mom takes her children's problems very personally," says Sue to her therapist. "I think this is because she knows, on some level, that she *wasn't* perfect. She knows we moved too often. She was a loving mom, but with Dad's drinking, we weren't the *perfect family*. I think it's too painful for Mom to look back."

There are many reasons why a family's emotional truths are dismissed, avoided, or denied by adults of all ages. Some of the most common reasons why people deny the truth are these:

> *The truth often hurts.*
> *The emotional "truth" (such as anger or dissatisfaction) is prohibited or viewed as "bad" according to family standards.*
> *The emotional truth may imply accusation and lead to parental guilt (whether justified or not).*
> *Emotional "truths" may not be based on verifiable facts.*
> *Mere ignorance.*

If a parent doesn't mirror back to the infant or youth what the child really feels, and doesn't respond appropriately, the adult child won't know how to label his or her own internal cues and put them to use.

If a parent punishes or psychologically threatens a child for honest feelings (like hating a baby sister or fearing an exam), the youth will learn to deny these feelings. If parents can't accurately label their *own* feelings, their adult children may have the same problem. In addition, their kids will misread the words and facial expressions of colleagues and friends. Later in life, these people may become depressed, guilty, or frightened when these prohibited emotions resurface.

The more upsetting the truth, the more intense the denial. Some people enter therapy after the death of a loved one, stating that they know they must be very sad; but they will avoid the subject of loss with grim determination. Eventually they admit that, should they start to "feel," they would never be able to stop crying. The more extreme or prohibited the pain, the more adamant a client will be about avoiding it. Parents of adults in therapy often operate on the same principle: "If the pot is hot, don't touch it!"

This is why family alcoholism, incest, and physical abuse commonly remain fixed family secrets. The damage to the victim and the consequences of exposure are serious. In most families with secrets of this sort, everyone unconsciously attempts to deny reality. When one family member (often a person in therapy) begins to "spill the beans," he or she may be labeled as crazy or be excommunicated altogether.

No one likes pain. However, the consequence of not confronting the pain and its source is a major cause of mental conflict, permanent psychic distress, and illness. Whether parents like it or not, their adult children in therapy must, at some point, confront the emotional realities of who they were as children and who they are now. The greatest gift you can offer your families at this point is honesty. You must not protect yourselves by lying to your children!

Delores

One day, Delores, a charming young beautician, asked me whether she should change careers. In this context, I inquired how she feels as she moves through a routine work day.

"But I didn't come here to find out what I *feel*!" she protested as she fiddled with her long blond curls.

"What did you come for?" I asked.

"I came for you to tell me whether I should change careers."

"And why don't you know this already?" I inquired.

"Because I don't know how I feel about anything any more."

Before delving deeper into emotional truths, I must emphasize that much of what a therapist and patient talk about does not involve loved ones. Therapy visits may be spent looking at everyday problems and the reasons why a person isn't solving them. The images of friends, lovers, bosses, social events, dreams, and fantasies drift through most therapy hours. Equally, the thoughts and inspirations acquired while listening to music or walking in nature enter the therapy dialogue. Central to the work I do is an ongoing discussion about what is happening here, in this room, between my patient and myself.

Claire

"I was furious at you when you told me last week that you'd be away on my birthday," raged Claire, a lonely young woman.

"Did I tell you I'd be away on your birthday?" I inquired with interest.

"Yes," said Claire. "You said you'd be away next Thursday. You are intentionally taking the day off because of my birthday," she added angrily.

Please note: I did not try to explain here that I had no idea next Thursday was her birthday. Far more central to this hour was Claire's angry perception that I would intentionally dismiss her on her birthday. Therefore, I wanted to know her feelings and thoughts—her emotional truths—about her birthday.

I said to Claire: "You have a lot of deep feelings about your birthday. Can you tell me more about all of this?"

"I sure hate birthdays," continued Claire, on the verge of tears. "Everyone forgets my birthday! No one sends cards. I always get depressed."

"Birthdays are painful for you," I reflected, feeling sad. "You wanted me to be here to share your birthday."

Claire began to weep. "Not just *wanted* to have you here! I was *counting* on having you here! Of all the days you are here, you won't be here when I need you most!"

Without apology, I mentioned to this lonely young woman that we would grow, with time, to understand why her birthdays were so exquisitely painful.

Two days later, Claire arrived and said, "I had the most amazing dream last night. In the dream I kept seeing five candles—like birthday candles—floating, taunting me in the darkness. In the dream I was very scared; I began to fall down a cliff. I fell and fell until I landed in a ravine. There was no one there to catch me.

"When I woke up, I was crying. Worst of all, I was remembering the time my folks went on vacation. I was very young, maybe five? They'd promised me they'd be back in time to celebrate my birthday. But something happened and they didn't get home. So I had my birthday with my sitter. When my parents returned, I never told them how upset I'd been. By now I'm so afraid of being overlooked that I don't even tell my friends my birth date—for fear they'll forget it."

Several days later Claire announced that since I wouldn't be in the office next week, she'd planned a luncheon party for herself. Not only were her best friends invited but also her parents—and all had accepted! It turned out to be one of the happiest birthdays Claire ever had.

Please note that when I was angrily attacked by Claire for "intentionally forgetting her birthday" I did not try to correct the fact that I had not even known of this upcoming event. If I had gotten into an "I never said" or "I never knew" defense, her central feelings about being "forgotten" would never have surfaced. In Claire's case, it was especially important to explore the meaning of her pain and to let the feelings emerge freely.

Feeling forgotten was the central theme of Claire's childhood, adulthood, and work with me. Feeling forgotten is what I call her *identity theme*. Claire's recovery of this childhood memory prompted more recollections of a similar sort. Because of her father's business trips and several deaths in the family, her parents had frequently been forced to travel out of town. Claire was always left with a sitter she did not like. But she'd never complained. Her birthday memory is what we call a "screen memory," or a vivid recollection representing earlier happenings of a similar nature.

As Claire began to realize that she sets herself up to be forgotten (for example, by not reminding her friends or her therapist when her birthday is imminent), she started to take better care of herself during potentially vulnerable times.

If a loved one in therapy makes reference to or attacks you for some painful event, you have many choices:

> *Flatly deny that the event ever happened.*
> *Criticize your loved one for remembering things "so wrong."*
> *Tell him or her that it's hurtful to be remembered so ungratefully.*
> *Say that, although you remembered the incident differently—or not at all—you would like to hear more about the situation.*

It takes courage to respond calmly when one feels unfairly, or worse, fairly attacked. However, if a parent wants to open channels of communication with a child, the parent must listen with an open heart to the child's emotional realities.

Parents want to believe they handled childcare well. It's easy to feel criticized or unappreciated when a child reproaches them about past or current mishaps. But, just as parents want children to respect their feelings, children want parents to respect theirs. The truth is always better than murky, withheld confusion. Parents may reach a new level of intimacy with children at any time if they learn to inquire and listen nondefensively—even if it hurts.

SIGNS OF GROWTH THROUGH LISTENING TO EMOTIONAL TRUTHS

Although my clients don't know it, I'm often touched by the efforts of their parents or partners to understand. I hear loved ones struggling to "make sense" of the changes, challenges, rages, and contradictions of their partners, sons and daughters. Although your loved ones may not admit it, they really know when you're trying to grasp their messages.

Jesse

Six years ago I worked twice weekly with a handsome physician who was raised in Tennessee. Jesse chose medicine as a career because, as a child, he had suffered life-threatening diabetes. He'd spent much of his childhood in the small local hospital, had nearly died several times, and had been a great burden to his attentive parents. Having been restricted from physical activity, he could never play sports. His identity theme was "the sickly child."

As a young adult, he tried to gain mastery over his physical limitations by helping others to recover from childhood diseases. He loved his work. But he was a miserably lonely and angry young man.

Although they were attentive to his illness, his family, like most families, was far from perfect. His father, an artist and athlete, could become sporadically explosive and hostile. His mother, a chemist, was religiously devout but exhausted—at all times—by the demands of Jesse's illness and the needs of her four other children. Their family had been under considerable stress. Jesse's parents lived far from relatives and had no one to help them with his "burdensome" health problems.

Jesse spent his first therapy year in tears. As Jesse would leave my office after each hour session, my waste basket would be overflowing with wet hankies.

Jesse was grieving the pain of his childhood.

"It was miserable. I was always afraid of getting sick, of eating too much or too little, of having to wake up my folks. I was afraid to go to sleep at night. Every night I'd pray, 'Please, Lord, don't let me get sick tonight. Please, Lord, don't make my parents angry if I do get sick tonight.' I never cried or complained aloud. I was told that if I got upset, I might get sick. So I held in the tears."

One of Jesse's complaints was the feeling that he'd been a "burden," and, therefore, must never feel angry at his parents. After all, he should be grateful. His parents—especially Dad—had frequently saved his life. How many times had Dad run from his studio with insulin or rushed Jesse to the emergency room? Dad had supplied him with special foods to take to school. Dad had not excelled as an artist perhaps because of the time it took to care for Jesse. So how could Jesse dare to complain?

Because of his illness, Jesse had been forced into unwanted dependency for far too long. Understandably, his parents had resented the constant demands he made on their lives, while at the same time trying to disguise their unhappy feelings.

In Jesse's second year of therapy, his tears turned to rage. Still he dared not voice anger at his parents although they lived nearby. After all, he felt he should be grateful and appreciative for all they'd done to keep him alive.

Jesse was outraged about his childhood. He was angry that he, not one of his brothers, was the sick kid. He felt that his parents had "taken care of the sickness and overlooked the child." He was angry that they'd gotten upset when he didn't watch his eating closely enough. His rage would surface most poignantly when, in visiting his parents, they would inquire about his health. Had he had a recent check-up? Was his insulin being regulated adequately?

"Who do they think I am? A sick kid?" protested this talented pediatrician.

Jesse's anger began to surface in relationship to anyone who stood in his way. "Slow lady drivers drive me nuts!" "That stupid medical student can't even draw blood!" "How dare the surgeon-chief not promote me to the senior staff? I will not be held back any more!"

At times Jesse's anger erupted at me:

"It's all your fault I'm messed up! I should be happy now! I've been seeing you for a year!"

As his anger increased, Jesse grew guilty and isolative. He rarely visited his parents for fear they would see his anger.

At times I sat and wondered what sense Jesse's folks were making of his obvious turmoil. Having told them that he was seeing a therapist, he occasionally received advisories from both his mother and father: "Now, don't let that therapist mess you up," they'd say. Or, "With the money you spend on her, you could buy a house!"

But Jesse and I knew that his primary problem was not just childhood diabetes. Illness had been a factor, but Jesse had phrased the problem well:

"My folks took care of the sick child, but forgot the child."

By this he meant, "They didn't have the time to know who I was as a person, as I lay in bed or was rushed to the hospital. I was never able to be me."

Jesse had difficulty seeing that, by now, his struggle was internal. He still yearned for the admiration of his parents. More importantly, he was at war with himself. His dreams indicated that he still saw himself as a skinny, sickly kid. He wanted to respect himself, but unconsciously had decided that he should suffer, that he *was* an unwanted burden.

Quite often, when people initiate therapy, they want to return to their parents to confront them, challenge them, and explain "the truth." This is a natural inclination and a sign that they are still dependent on their parents. They yearn for total parental understanding. This impulse is especially common among young patients at the beginning of treatment because the problem has not yet been accepted as internal.

Still in his twenties, with the memories of childhood as fresh as yesterday, Jesse wanted to force his parents to understand his suffering, yet he continued to dread their hurt, angry reactions. After all, of all the children, he should be the most grateful.

One gray Thursday morning, Jesse announced that he was writing an important letter to his dad. I found out that during the past three months he'd written nine drafts. "I'm writing to Dad because Dad's the one who might understand," he stated. "Furthermore, Mother's sensitive to criticism; she cries if she feels unappreciated."

Although I had not recommended that he write the letter, Jesse's compulsive rewriting of the document conveyed a desperate urge to "make Dad understand." I inwardly shivered as I thought how his father would feel after reading the letter. Nevertheless, I listened intently while attempting to understand, clarify, and respect this young man's anguished labor.

In the letter, Jesse emphasized that although his dad had been a loving parent, Jesse had felt like a sickly burden. He wanted his dad to know that he was miserable and in therapy because he'd had a disastrous childhood. He would explain his anger about not being able to go on family trips, and about spending so much time in the hospital. He would tell Dad that all he wanted was his dad's respect and understanding.

The tenth draft completed, Jesse arrived in my office feeling elated.

"Well, I sent the letter!" he pronounced victoriously. Again, I privately shuddered. "All I want from Dad is understanding. I just want him to say: 'Wow! It was rougher for you than I thought! It must have been awful to be left out so much!'"

"I feel like celebrating!" triumphed Jesse. "I finally wrote the perfect letter! I just know Dad will understand!"

Six days later Jesse arrived in my office and exploded into angry tears. He'd received a call from his father and a card from his mother.

First, Jesse was furious at me: "You should never have let me send that letter!" he moaned. "I'm angry that you let me send that letter."

Although I had never recommended that he write or send the letter, I quietly asked what had happened.

"Well, first Dad called to invite me to lunch. He said he'd received my letter and that I'd become all mixed up. He said he was disturbed by my lack of gratitude, and that my mother had been in tears all night. He also wanted me to know that I was a 'loved child.'"

"You weren't satisfied with your dad's response?" I asked.

"Of course not! All I wanted to hear was that Dad could understand how I felt."

Jesse doubled over, enraged. "All I wanted was to hear him say, 'Wow! It must have been rough.'

"Then I got this card from Mom. And although I know she's trying, the card made matters worse."

I asked Jesse what his mother had said.

"It wasn't what *she* said, but what the card said," responded Jesse.

"And what did the card say?"

"It was a store-bought card with a little jingle on the front. A totally meaningless jingle like:

Be merry and glad
Be merry and glad
Just look at the good
And not at the bad.
As long as you want
True love to last
You must live in the present
And not in the past.

"Then she just signed her name, 'Love, Mom.'

"If only they knew how hard I have tried to be happy and forget. But the memories keep haunting me—no matter how hard I try to preoccupy myself. My parents absolutely cannot understand; and they never ever will!" Jesse's angry tears turned into renewed depression.

I, not Jesse, could appreciate his parents' efforts to respond to their injured son. They had reached out in the best way they knew: to reassure their son of their love and to encourage a positive outlook.

By now, however, love was not enough. Jesse needed to have his feelings mirrored back to him as legitimate. Had his parents known this, I presume they would have done just that.

But how were they to know? No one had ever told them when they were growing up that their feelings were important.

For awhile, Jesse's parents were challenged by the turbulent separation process of their son. Although I never met them, I could feel his parents' confusion, hurt, and frustration as they attempted to respond to his contradictory communications.

They were reacting, in part, to Jesse's delayed rebellion. In order to move on with life, Jesse had work to do. Among his tasks, he needed to grieve his losses, such as the fantasy of ever having had a happy, healthy childhood. Jesse also needed time to establish confident independence since he had been medically dependent on his parents throughout adolescence. Could he ever relinquish the childhood dream of becoming his parents' favorite son—fully healthy and athletic? In essence, Jesse was moving through the steps of an active, delayed adolescent rebellion.

Susan Littwin's book, *The Postponed Generation: Why American Youth Are Growing Up Late,* describes the complexity of becoming psychologically separate. Littwin states that from the psychological perspective, "Rebellion is a reaction to dependency. The dependent person feels angry, acts it out, and then needs to be rescued, thus tying his parents to him. Once again, he is their helpless child."

Happily, Jesse was fiercely motivated to heal himself in all ways. Although his parents were frequently confused by his messages and temporary withdrawal from the family, I knew that they, too, were committed (as they always had been) to his well-being. Yes, they criticized his therapy and therapist for "messing him up." And this did, indeed, increase Jesse's frustrations. They were often unable to "mirror back" his feelings as legitimate. If they had been able to do this, Jesse and his family could have reunited sooner.

However, from my perspective, Jesse's parents never gave up. They continued to call, to send notes, and to respond with sensitivity to some of his requests. Although they were never able to say, "Yes, you had a miserable childhood," they did start listening. On one occasion it was his mother, not his father, who broke into tears, saying, "How hard it must have been for you. You looked so small and lonely whenever we left you in the hospital!"

At Jesse's request (through a letter), his parents stopped asking him about his health and started asking about his job. They also stopped stressing the importance of marriage. Instead, they asked about his friends. As Jesse became less revengeful and more able to communicate, his parents became more verbal about their own life stories. As Jesse learned more about them, his parents' patterns of responding began to make more sense. For example, his father confided that he'd lost a sister when he was a child. He told Jesse that his extreme tension, irritability, and over-protectiveness were partly because he could not tolerate the terrifying thought of another loss.

As Jesse's energies shifted from those of a tormented child and angry adolescent, he became eager to make life work for him. He developed friends and new interests which he carried home with him.

Jesse's parents were strongly affected by their son's therapeutic journey into adulthood. As they grew in their ability to reflect back to Jesse the legitimacy of his emotional truths, Jesse no longer confronted them with their "inability to understand." He became a fully active adult who could think about his parents' needs and happily say, "Thanks, folks!"

Postscript: I recently received a letter from Tennessee. In it, Jesse described his recent marriage and relocation to his parents' small town. He's working as a pediatrician at the local clinic while overseeing his parents' property. His mother has been suffering from severe arthritis and he's decided it's time— as a doctor—to really thank his folks. "Time to take care of ma and pa now! Best wishes, Jess."

I have highlighted the issue of emotional honesty, because it is one common theme that makes its way through therapy hours and back to the family or relationship. Because emotional truths are so central to the work of a person in psychotherapy, I will return to this concept in a later chapter.

Regardless of the form of therapy you or your adult child

selects, emotional truths will always be the subtext of your family's history. If your husband says he's angry because of an insult at work, it would be beneficial to talk through the incident with him and try to understand its meaning. If you visit your daughter-in-law and she says she feels embarrassed about the condition of her house, you might say that although you're sorry she feels this way, you are so glad to have been invited! If a good friend says that as a child he often felt like second best, why not ask him to tell you more?

We all want to be understood. Our attempts to listen and understand convey our love.

CHAPTER 4

THE FACE OF SEPARATENESS

If we are always arriving and departing, it is also true that we are eternally anchored. One's destination is never a place, but rather a new way of looking at things.

Henry Miller

"Jake has changed since he's been in therapy," objected Jake's mother, Betsy, to her daughter. "He used to be so polite, so kind. He was such a sweet little boy! Now he's reserved, almost cold. I sure hope that psychiatrist isn't putting bad ideas into his head!"

"Don't worry, Mom," responded Marge, who had also been in therapy. "Jake just needs time to find himself."

"*Find himself!*" replied Betsy briskly. "He's almost thirty-two! I liked him better the way he was."

Unfortunately for Betsy, Jake's no longer trying to be her "sweet" little boy. Raised among "too many hovering women," he is trying to distance himself from maternal pleas that he be "sweet as pumpkin pie." His passive, apologetic, ingenuine submissiveness isn't working in his favor any more.

But Betsy doesn't like the changes. She feels worried and betrayed.

"I just hope that therapist doesn't ruin him," she protested again.

The process of becoming emotionally separate (while maintaining human relations) is not new to the younger generation. Throughout history, people have sung the songs of leaving their parents, their homes. In societies which offer *rites of passage* to their young adults, months of preparation precede the grand and official departure from childhood. These rites of passage are socially approved, predictable, and proudly celebrated by the entire community.

Just fifty years ago in our own society, youths were whisked more rapidly into forced forms of separateness. "I had a full-time mechanic's job at nineteen," explains Jake's father, Dan, with robust pride. "I had a wife and son by the age of twenty. I helped my parents in their bakery. Back then we didn't have time to think about all this separation stuff." It's true Dan might not have thought about becoming separate when he was young. Perhaps that's why he unknowingly repeated with his children the harsh parenting behaviors he most disliked in his father.

Today, adults in therapy want to take the time to maximize their potentials as separate, unique people. Psychologically-minded and resourceful, they are practicing a new art form: the art of finding out who they really want to be. Faced with too many choices, young people may erupt with urgent force during these explorations. Adults in therapy want to maximize their potentials for work, love, and play. They may be just as busy—or busier— than people fifty years ago, but many feel the need to reflect on their lives and choices in disciplined ways.

Sometimes parents object to therapy and blame the therapist for the seemingly sudden changes they witness in their children. But what they're really protesting may be the loss of what is familiar—including the loss of the adult child's singular loyalty. Comfort resides in sameness. Thus many parents and loved ones cling to familiar but dangerous patterns of behavior despite their earnest initial efforts to change. Despite our natural human tendency to adapt, an equally powerful force lures us back to the familiar. Many parents unknowingly want their children back unchanged. "I liked Jake better the way he was," Betsy said sadly to her daughter..

For some adults, the therapy journey is a condensed and comparatively rapid time for psychological hatching. What might have taken twenty years (or never have occurred at all) is consolidated into one or more years of therapy, so the parents, friends, and loved ones of people in therapy have reason to feel perplexed.

Lacking the clinician's profound conviction that patients can create more gratifying lives, parents see only isolated signs that highlight an adult child's "differentness." Awkward abruptness, moodiness, emotional withdrawal, confrontations, questioning, or absenteeism from the family flock are among the temporary signs of significant internal change. Unable to relax, some parents don't trust that their sons and daughters will find their ways back home. Highly attuned to the work in progress, they fear they won't like the final product of therapy.

FAMILY FIRST? THE "BLURRED SELF"

"There's this blurring between my family and myself," says Camille, a bright law student. It's hard to describe, but there's this group called the Robinsons; and what the Robinsons believe, is what the Robinsons believe. It's always been 'family first' in our family. That's what Dad has said for years. And it's such a nice idea, but when I have separate interests, or different values, I get confused. It's almost as if the 'me' disappears."

Camille, at thirty-three, is highly conflicted about who the "real Camille" is. The state of feeling merged, blurred, or without a center can be terrifying. This frightening emotional experience, if chronic, can lead to psychological numbing and feelings of being emotionally dead, lifeless, and lost. Previously enjoyed activities and goals no longer have meaning. I want to stress the immobilizing aspects of the "lost self" because it is a state of being that you, as parents and loved ones of people in therapy, may not be able to relate to.

When one feels separate or autonomous, one feels clear, energetic, directed. Being psychologically distinct is a state of being many people take for granted. "I always knew I wanted to be a homemaker," claims Camille's artistic mother. "I've always been a fisherman at heart!" declares her father. Mr. and Mrs. Robinson, since adolescence, knew who they were and what they wanted. As did their parents, they attended church proudly and expected their only daughter to do the same. It's often difficult for parents such as the Robinsons to understand the driving, complicated urge of their children to "find themselves."

To be "out of touch" with oneself is an old expression with true psychological roots. A mentally protective wall has been erected to ward off emotions or conflicts which threaten the person's sense of internal organization. Because unconscious processes shield the adult from unwanted or painful emotions, a skilled clinician works gently while attempting to label and understand new feelings in small doses.

When an adult begins to hatch from a numbed state, new emotional experiences also emerge: tears, anger, disappointment, protest, gratitude. Slowly, and with increasing insight, the adult client comes alive. Unfamiliar sets of emotions can erupt like volcanoes. Although initially disruptive, these new feelings propel rapid change. Previously denied feelings (and the thoughts that accompany them) serve as guides when considering major life decisions.

Intense feelings typically unnerve the loved ones of people in therapy. Sometimes these emotions are "not nice." To parents' horror, sons and daughters may express the very same feelings that they were carefully taught *not* to feel, such as anger or jealousy. We can therefore understand why parents openly object to these early signs of self-definition.

Camille initiated treatment for reasons she could only vaguely describe. In her first consultation she confessed, "It's as if I just don't know who I am any more. I'm about to finish law school, but I feel out of touch with myself. I'm uncomfortable—kind of nervous, kind of numb." Camille stared at me through blandly blank eyes. She was petite and trim, and wore a blue scarf over her braided black hair.

As her life story unfolded, Camille learned that she had been, and still was, a "parenting child." Until her third year of law school, she felt total responsibility for her parents' happiness. One weekend each month, Camille drove three hours to her parents' home in a small fishing village. Camille believed that her generous but lonely parents "lived" for her trips home.

However, Camille had not yet discovered that she would feel lonely if she alienated herself from her parents. Her compulsive need to care for her parents reflected her own insecurity as an independent adult. For example, her self respect and sense of well-being were singularly dependent on her parents' approval.

She complained that she was in a "no win" situation. If she didn't visit her parents, Camille felt guilty, unfaithful, confused, and lonely. If she did visit them, she always returned to my office feeling lost, blurred, and unsure of who she was. Frightened about her entry into the cosmopolitan world of lawyers, angry at her parents for what she perceived was neediness, and hateful towards herself for her failure to take charge of herself, Camille felt that her childhood vitality had evaporated.

Camille's story is just one of thousands which exemplify the young adult's precarious inward journey towards independence. Mr. and Mrs. Robinson were caught in the middle. Unaware of their daughter's inner turmoil, they started to wonder why Camille rarely called. When they did talk to Camille, she was often brief, unfriendly, and irritable. Confused about her temporary choice to visit less often, they finally asked, "Have we done something to offend you?"

"Oh, no," responded Camille, not wanting to hurt her parents' feelings. "I'm just busy studying."

In my office Camille tried to explain what she felt when she visited her parents:

"It's like, there's a family viewpoint. Like, *the Robinsons go to Mass every Sunday—together*. This is a lovely idea. I love Mass, unless I'm exhausted. If I'm with my parents and have been up all night studying, I want to sleep late on Sunday. But *the Robinsons go to Mass every Sunday*. Dad wakes up and hollers, 'Time for Mass!' I feel that God would want me to rest, but Dad keeps calling: 'Mass time! Mass time!' So I feel angry at him, guilty about wanting sleep, and sacrilegious for feeling that God could understand. It's like running into a brick wall, because family values come first, and I don't know where the 'me' fits in. I begin to feel myself melting away. I feel very unsure of myself. I begin to grow numb, blurred. You have to stay a Robinson through and through to be part of the fold."

There are many reasons why adults today struggle for self-sufficiency in such unique and conflicted ways. For example, Camille, while retaining her family's religious beliefs, had difficulty relinquishing her childhood need to soothe her depressed parents, who had wanted a large family but conceived only once. Terrified of injuring her adoring parents, Camille could never tell them about her feelings or confusion; her resentment, despair, and irritation were thinly veiled, however. During her therapy, Camille was so defiantly protective of her parents that she never gave them the chance to understand why she was suddenly so distant. Like sea sponges, Mr. and Mrs. Robinson absorbed her depressive withdrawal. They would retire at night, hurt and confused, asking each other, "Did we do something to offend Camille?"

The answer was "no." Their daughter was becoming her own woman.

SEPARATENESS FROM THE PSYCHOLOGICAL PERSPECTIVE

There are a number of sociological causes for the prolonged separation processes of adult children. Since examining social trends is simpler than exploring the complex internal processes of psychological evolution, let's briefly review some environmental stressors which influence adults of all ages.

Later Marriages

Jean Okimoto and Phyllis Stegall observe that "in 1960, 72 percent of women between the ages of twenty and twenty-four were married. In 1984, only 43 percent of women in that age group were married. There has been almost a 50 percent drop in the marriage rate of young adults compared to their parents' generation. And among Americans aged thirty to thirty-five, the percentage of people who have never married has doubled since 1970."

A large portion of the young adult population has not yet "partnered." Whether heterosexual or gay, some adults are content with single life and relish the freedom of independence. Others, having seen friends and parents divorce, doubt the value of promises and marriage.

"Do you know of any marriages that last?" demanded my client Steve. Before I could answer, Steve blurted, "Well, by now I view marriage as a myth! My dad's been married three times and my mom—twice. None of my friends' folks are together and none of us believe in marriage. So, Dr. Spencer, do you know of any successful marriages?"

Anxious fights often erupt between the newly engaged—especially when wedding or holy union dates are announced. These people are scared. Having witnessed the marital catastrophes of parents and peers, many people like Steve are skeptical. Others become obsessively perfectionistic about partnership choices. Without a partner, the single adult remains awkwardly (if not angrily) dependent on the original family for emotional support. Parents, although respectful of their offspring's full adulthood, serve as their children's guardians for an exceptionally long time. Sometimes they grow weary of this role. "I've paid my dues!" exclaimed Mrs. Liverinston, age sixty. "When will I have my house to myself?"

Divorce

According to Okimoto and Stegall, young adults who are children of divorced parents undoubtedly had some difficult or unsettling childhood experiences. They state further that divorce often plays a key role in delayed separation between parents and children. Knowing that they've hurt their kids by getting divorced, these parents may try to compensate in any way they can. Often, when adult children want to return home, the parents will take them in unconditionally.

Left with the unconscious wish to reunite their parents, some children of divorce must face and then grieve this hopeless fantasy. Others are terrified of abandonment. Adult children often become extremely tense when their separated parents and their parents' new partners join forces (such as at graduations and weddings) and think back nostalgically on intact family gatherings. Many children of divorce seek therapy because they lack internal images of loyal, contented relationships. As stated by my client Kristin, "When I think of marriage I visualize two warships attacking each other!" Fantasies about "real families" contrast painfully with memories of being left alone or shuffled from parent to parent. Jose, another client of mine, lamented, "What *is* a family? I grew up with Dad and rarely visited Mom. Now that I'm twenty-one, Mom keeps talking about getting the 'family' together. I keep telling her, 'Mom, we're not a family!' She claims that we *are* a family. Who's she talking about? Her and me? We were never a family!"

In many neighborhoods where extended families are the norm, powerful single mothers or fathers are admired both as community leaders and dynamic parents. There is no "one best way" to raise a family or to welcome our youth into adulthood; many children bear single parenting and divorce with robust grace. Still, others harbor deep insecurities. At holiday times these youths anxiously weep while deciding whether to eat turkey with their mothers or their fathers. With only childhood fantasies and television images to guide them, children of divorce need time to create realistic life goals. They need the strength, availability, and patience of their parents and loved ones. Your tolerance for their emotional outbursts can help them as they strive for what feels impossible. Sometimes the most trusted or involved parent becomes the target of intense rage. Keep this in mind as you listen to your adult children and convey that you're trying to understand.

Too Few Rituals

"I'm planning a block party for the day Gerald returns from his trip to L.A.!" announced Mrs. Petit, who lives in a small town in West Virginia.

"From L.A.?" I asked.

"Yes! Driving across the country is like an American safari for him. He's driving out and back to prove he's a man! He's worked odd jobs to pay for gas and food. So—I'm welcoming him home with a block party. Just wait till he drives down the street in his '84 pickup and sees the streamers and potato salad! It'll be *his* day!" Mrs. Petit was excited.

Western society today does not provide any of the rituals that once welcomed unmarried young adults into full maturity. What "new" rituals can you design to publicly acknowledge your sons' and daughters' passages into adulthood?

Economic Boomerangs and Intergenerational Living

A generation ago young people could afford to rent an apartment or get married right out of school. The economy, however, has changed dramatically, as has the cost of living. College and graduate school tuitions have skyrocketed. Today's young adults can't look forward to starting incomes that allow them both housing and pleasant lifestyles.

Although financing the adult world may seem an impossible assignment and the difficulties may "boomerang" our young adults back home, these people can still live harmoniously with their parents. Many societies enjoy intergenerational households which, as we know, are becoming increasingly common in America. If all family members make mutually respectful contributions to household tasks and finances, living intergenerationally can provide rich opportunities for renewing ties with children and grandparents. Problems arise, however, if children returning home aren't required to claim full responsibility for their adult roles within the family. Also, if parents have difficulties acknowledging their adult children as mature, distinct, and fully competent, the benefits of this living arrangement will be compromised.

"How can I tell Dad I don't like his insults when I know he'd retaliate by withdrawing my tuition or kicking me out of the house?" asked a twenty-five year old computer programmer.

Although money doesn't truly represent the "tie that binds," it may bend your children into submission, dependence, hypocritical obligation, or inhibition in relationship to you. Must our kids pay emotional wages for our financial gifts? Generosity means freedom, liberation of the spirit. Can we grant assistance to our young adults without resentful grudges or binding controls? If giving a gift makes you feel genuinely joyous, you're also giving yourself a gift. True gifts are acts of love rendered without strings or retaliatory afterthoughts.

Money matters tie adult children to their parents. Nevertheless, money—and the spirit with which it is rendered and received—aren't the only issues which matter.

Material Versus Spiritual Values

Okimoto and Stegall contend that the last twenty years have been marked by a society "that worshiped 'the right stuff,' not the stuff of character, but things and more things: the right label, the right brand, the right make, the right model, the right name, the right *stuff* . . ." Such desires are often unattainable for young people starting out.

It's well-known that many women, for financial or personal reasons, worked outside the home when their children were young. These mothers suffered internal conflicts, especially guilt, about their careers. "Am I spending enough time with my child?" is still a common question. Because of this guilt, many parents attempted to undo their "wrongs" by buying their children the right stuff. Television, promoting the right brand, became the baby sitter and value setter for many of today's young adults.

Do our adult children represent a discouraged population that can no longer afford "the good things of life?" Financial problems force young folks to work. But lack of the right material "stuff" isn't really what makes our young adults feel impoverished. Instead, the absence of soothing, encouraging parents fosters profound insecurity as young adults face their choices and challenges. Ongoing experiences with one or more supportive parents are essential to our children's success with life's tests.

"My mom never sends me money," says college sophomore Diane. "As kids, we didn't have fancy things—and never ate out. So I don't expect the things that other students want. But I never felt poor. My mom's great. She's a seamstress and sends my roommates hand-knit scarves. I never question whether I'm loved. It's as if Mom is always with me when I take tests—like, she's saying, 'I'm praying for you, honey; you can do it.'"

With the many choices put before adults of all ages—including decisions about whether drug use can fill an emotional void—young adults need heavy doses of encouragement, reassurance, and love. We all seek protection from violence, crime, AIDS, and environmental hazards. As parents and older adults, we can convey confidence to our youth that they can survive and find meaning in their lives. The stamina and spiritual values we model to young adults send messages of hope.

Some people carry themselves with grace from a very young age. They may be sturdy, caring, and wise. Approaching school and career with energy and optimism, many gifted people enjoy the rewards of having had happy, challenging childhoods. So, when these "super-kids" glide into a psychotherapist's office, they display faces of dismay.

"I can't believe I called you," said Don, a popular young science teacher. He sat forward, elbows propped on sturdy knees. Unable to hide his tears, he shook his head in confusion. "I had great parents, a great childhood. I like my job and have *always* wanted to be a teacher, but things aren't working out as

I'd expected. I'm not happy, not happy at all. I feel disappointed about something, like something's missing. But I don't know what it is."

Don's embarrassed tears expressed the surprise of a talented man who grew up too soon. Raised by overly earnest parents to take on responsibilities beyond his years, he'd never had time to be a little boy. With play and spontaneity absent from his childhood, Don had styled himself around a demanding work ethic.

Unknowingly, Don had developed a pattern of "shooting for the next ladder, the next goal, the next prize." Therefore, after meeting all his preestablished destinies (a challenging job, a loving wife), he felt bereft. No more awards, no more prizes. "Just me."

When Don entered treatment, he had already decided that if a man "had a happy childhood, he wouldn't need professional help."

Not true. As many novels and movies demonstrate, happy beginnings do not guarantee happy endings. Therapists often hear these words: "Everything was going so well until . . ."

SEPARATENESS FROM THE PSYCHOLOGICAL PERSPECTIVE

The Celebrations of Separateness

Separateness wears many happy faces:

Can you remember when you were awarded that first promotion because you did a great job? How about the time you showed your mother your new home? Filled with pride, you walked her through the colorful rooms—all tidy and polished for her congratulations!

There is a wonderful feeling that comes from seeing a handicapped child push her wheelchair all by herself through the Special Olympics games with crowds cheering her.

Your baby's first words and steps were subject matter for photos and videotapes. The news you describe in holiday letters pronounces your separate successes and joys.

Where does the expression "nothing to write home about" come from? It's derived from our urgent need to "make something" of ourselves. The expression conveys concern that our parents might not otherwise be totally impressed.

Don't we "cheer" each other on all the time with the challenges of separate living? Arriving at milestones in our lives, despite all hurdles, is true cause for celebration. Why? Because as we all know, life is difficult. Our accomplishments enjoy the applause of admirers.

I have never worked with a parent who did not want his or her adult child to feel gratified by life. Yet, at the same time, we rarely celebrate our own accomplishments as parents. Of course, parents sometimes have difficulty acknowledging their parental mistakes, but many parents have a tendency to look almost exclusively at their failings, faults, and all those times they weren't "there" for their children. This self-punishing tendency leads to a lack of celebration for all that was freely offered and sacrificed.

Therefore, as we approach the next section, which highlights several special problems of adult children, I hope, if you are a parent, you will actively keep in mind your constructive and high-spirited efforts to cheer your children through infinite numbers of developmental tasks. My purpose here is not to offer an in-depth discussion of the life cycle and its ongoing phases of separation and reconnection. Instead, I want to help you to understand the separation process as it relates to your adult child's therapy journey.

I'll try to de-mystify your loved one's therapy process for you. When clinicians work with children and young adolescents, they often work with parents and family members as well. This way, everyone participates and understands the nature of the basic problem. Neither the therapists nor the therapy hour is mysterious. Family therapy also allows relatives to discuss shared concerns together.

Understand, however, that if you're the relative of an adult in individualized treatment, you may not be invited to attend regular meetings. Some therapists will be delighted, at your son's or daughter's request, to meet with you for a joint meeting. Others believe that the inclusion of friends and family members disrupts and/or complicates the adult client's work. If your sons or daughters are trying to distinguish their ideas and goals from yours, you probably won't be invited to participate.

Still, you will be a participant from afar, because of the ripple effect we mentioned earlier. You may or may not be aware of the subtle or radical changes in your child or partner. On some level, however, you'll eventually benefit from their efforts to take charge of their lives and increase their capacities for work, love, and play.

The next sections exemplify a number of situations in which family members are affected by challenges of self-determination and the therapy process. Even if you are not able to identify yourself or your adult child in any one scene, you'll surely see similarities between yourself, people you know, and the following examples.

THE TOO-PERFECT, TOO-CLOSE-FOR-COMFORT PARENT

Marley and Her Mom

Marley Hill stopped at her mother's house to drop off the borrowed vacuum cleaner. Says her mother, "You don't look like you feel well, honey. Come on in for some tea."

"Gotta go, Mom," Marley responds with irritation.

"But, dear, you're working too hard. And you don't look happy. What's wrong?"

"Mom, will you get off my case!" shrieks Marley. "You're always making these wild assumptions and you ask too many questions!"

Feeling hurt and dismissed, Marley's mother closes the door as Marley drives away. "What did I do wrong this time?" she asks herself as she wearily goes back to drying the dishes.

Well, Marley's mother didn't do anything "wrong." Her child just isn't inviting her on board. Marley's irritation is unconsciously prompted by the wish and the fear that she just might take refuge on her mom's couch, break into tears, and tell her mom about problems with her boyfriend. As Marley describes it, "I can't let myself stay at home for long or else I'll regress, feel like a child, want to stay forever, and lose the energy to keep going."

Can you remember when your toddler was beginning to talk? From the toddler's perspective, you just couldn't do anything right. The baby grunts and points. "Is it the apple you want?" you ask lovingly, fetching the fruit from the fridge. The child tries again, showing frustration and anger while pointing harder. "Is it the bottle? The truck? The cookie?" By trial and error you keep trying to satisfy his desire, but you can't decipher his message. All the while, the child is screaming louder. Finally, you give up, leaving the outraged toddler to struggle with his limitations. He shakes and shrieks, trying to communicate something that is beyond his verbal reach. You really did your best, but the baby wasn't ready. Through frustrations like these, though, he learned new words and eventually mastered the art of communication.

Think of the halting, sometimes angry, messages of your adult children in therapy. There's a lot that they haven't yet defined for themselves. They're confused about why they're depressed, insecure, angry, or anxious. They don't know why their angry outbursts have shocked their supervisors or why they can't make a single relationship last. They don't know yet.

Even if they do know, however, they wouldn't want to regress to your worried, fearful, needy, grasping embrace, however loving it might be. Running back to you is not part of the assignment called "growing separate." At least, not for now.

Marley, who grouchily returned her mother's vacuum cleaner, had always enjoyed a loving relationship with her mother. In fact, this very closeness became one of the reasons for her occasional outbursts at the woman she still admired.

Marley and her mother had shared the good and the sad times. After Mrs. Hill was abandoned by her alcoholic husband when Marley was three, she raised her daughter alone. Mrs. Hill gave careful attention to every detail of Marley's youth. She made Marley's clothes and ironed each dress with precision. Marley never "looked poor." Her mother never missed a school performance or a chance to help Marley with her studies. In addition, Mrs. Hill worked night shifts at the nearby hospital. An intelligent and determined laboratory technician, she dedicated her entire adult life to the loving care of her daughter. And what a beautiful young woman Marley became! Marley had gained inner strength and competence by watching (and identifying with) her mother. Marley's personhood reflected many of her mother's coping skills, interests, and artistic preferences.

However, when Marley reached twenty, she felt an unexpected tension while spending time with her mother. "I guess we were just too close for comfort," Marley commented to her therapist. "You just can't be that close to a mom and move out on your own. I worry about Mom a lot. I think about her living alone in that tiny house with no one to talk to." Marley began to weep. "It's so hard to leave her all alone. I almost hold my breath and bolt to get out of the house. I know Mom too well, and I know she's lonely. She doesn't push or intrude. She's never done that. Yet in my heart, I feel a pressure.

"I miss Mom," continued Marley sadly. "Sometimes I'd like to be a child again, snuggled in her lap. On the other hand, it feels too close for comfort."

Fortunately, Marley's mother, although uncertain about how to proceed with her own life, senses these struggles within her daughter. She does not burden Marley with her own problems because it's time for Marley to establish *her* own place in the world. Will Mrs. Hill find a way to remap her life?

Many young adults struggle with the "too-close-for-comfort" parent. Most youths may push away the parent of the opposite sex. Rarely aware of the sexual tensions they feel, hugging the opposite-sex parent can be "too close for comfort." Thus adoring mothers may be temporarily ignored by their robust sons, and attentive fathers, previously worshiped, may be undercut or dismissed by their vivacious daughters.

How can a parent know whether he or she is "too close for comfort?" If the parent feels pushed away, they're too close! A daughter may reproach a mother for lack of fashion sense, the way her mother relates to her, and generally having different interests. She may withdraw for long periods in an effort to establish her own identity. Then one day to the parent's surprise, she arrives on the doorstep as if she'd never been away. She may forget her mother's birthday, or forget to return the same mother's favorite pot! It just might be that, at least subconsciously, she enjoys the comfort of cooking in that skillet behind the parent's back.

Sons and daughters who feel too close for comfort in relationship to their parents do a dance all their own. They'll push the parent way, then slide back.

This is not a fun dance.

Ralph and His Dad

"You pushed me too hard when I was a boy, Dad. You'll never give up the fantasy that I'll be a superstar like you!" Ralph lashed out at his super-dad over the dinner table.

His father, who was carving the roast, looked up, stunned. He had encouraged, supported, and yes, pushed his son to "be the best," or, at least, the best he could be. He'd never missed any of Ralph's basketball games.

Yet Ralph, in reviewing his sports participation with his therapist, shrank back in horror. "I was hardly ever put in the game, and when I was, I got so scared that I rarely scored."

Having admired, if not idealized his father, Ralph was finally facing his own limitations. "Dad was too perfect a dad. He always knew how to fix things. He was always on time. He had good values and a high-paid job. He always shouted out 'You're the best!' I'd like to be like Dad, I think. Or would I? I'm confused. Inside my brain I've got this tape that says 'Be your *best*, Son! Be the best you can be!' But sometimes I grow tired of trying to be my best. A lot of the time, I don't think my best is very good. If only Dad hadn't pushed me so hard," fretted Ralph, "it would be easier to be me."

While Ralph was struggling to accept his limitations he was also consoling himself that his father wasn't so perfect. Had his father failed him by being "too perfect?"

Be prepared for scrutiny if you're a too-close or too-perfect parent. Many adult children's scrutinies of their parents will be private. Children, feeling too tightly bound, may admire the parent just a bit too much. Despite their criticisms, they also have idealized images of who the parent is. Despite their confusion as to reality, there's comfort in the concept of an all-loving, all-perfect, all-protective father or mother.

The too-close or too-perfect parent can overwhelm a

young person's sense of personal identity and value. A son's silent withdrawal can hurt the parent, especially if the mother or father's self-esteem is invested in the absolute success of the child or the parent's perfectionist identity.

If a parent is a "too-perfect" or "too-close-for-comfort" parent, the mother or father needn't retaliate by withdrawing interest in their children's lives. By trying to understand the messages of young people's challenges, the parent will maintain his or her identity. Finding new projects and other people in whom to invest your energy will help the parent and offspring to release themselves from a relationship that is too close for comfort. Let sons and daughters know that parents, too, made plenty of mistakes. Be specific! Give examples of promotions that didn't come, pies that fell, and other disappointments large and small.

The Unleapable Chasm: Far-Away Parents

Rick

"I worked like a dog for a week," Rick says to his therapist. " I wanted to get my new condo ready for Mom and Dad's visit. Cecile helped. We scrubbed the floors and stayed up till midnight painting the guest room. I wanted my place to be perfect.

"I had this plan, since what I wanted most was to connect with Dad. Cecile would take Mom to her office, and Dad and I would play golf. Dad relaxes when he plays golf.

"They arrived, they admired the house, and then my old emptiness set in. Dad turned on the television. As always, he held the remote control in his hand. During every ad he kept flicking the channels, back and forth, back and forth. So Mom, Cecile, and I went to the kitchen and talked. Cecile kept looking at me because she knew I was getting depressed. I kept the conversation going, but I felt hurt and angry. I went back to the living room and said, 'Pop, how about a game of golf?' 'Thanks, son,' he said, but I'm pretty tired from the drive.'

"'How about chess?'" I tried again. Surfing the channels, Dad replied, 'Nice idea, maybe later.' I know Dad was tired, but he's always been tired—and glued to the tube.

"With Dad there seems to be this unleapable chasm that will never be crossed. He's a decent man, but distant. I don't think I'll ever feel close to Dad. Sometimes I feel like screaming, 'Hey, man, can't you talk?' But he wouldn't get it.

"Dad's a far-away man—out of reach. I feel lonely when I think about Dad. That's why I keep trying to get through to him. I keep thinking, there must be a way."

Among Rick's reasons for entering therapy was the lifelong wish that he could "get through to Dad." He was the middle son and not the one chosen by his father to be his golf partner. Big brother and Dad would take off for the course on Sundays while Rick was left at home to "keep Mom company."

Without knowing it, Rick had strongly identified with his father. Like his father, Rick was depressive, passive, and somberly distant before starting therapy. Commonly, a child becomes intensely identified (for example, in terms of character traits and behavioral patterns) with the more depriving or frightening parent. This unconscious process aids the helpless child to feel internally powerful in a hopeless relationship.

By the time Rick was twenty-nine, he'd become so indecisive that he often spent twenty minutes deciding which tie to wear. His childhood wish to change his father and at the same time relate to him entered every therapy hour. Obsessed at times with his thoughts about his father, this sad young man couldn't focus his energy on self-directed tasks. His unmet needs for an engaging father figure kept him standing still in a hollow of unhappiness.

During one phase of therapy Rick decided he needed to

"fix" his relationship with his father. He started sending news clippings about topics of interest to his father: the latest football statistics, updates on golf pros, and some barbecue recipes. But his father rarely made reference to these invitations for dialogue.

During another phase of therapy Rick decided to confront his father. "Hey, Dad! I'm mad that you never answered my letters," he pronounced. "You only talk about sports or my brothers. You never ask about my job or Cecile." At this point his father swung around from the television set.

"Since when do we talk to each other this way?" questioned Dad. "Of course I'm interested in you!" He turned back to the television screen, but he stopped flicking the channels. He appeared to be lost in thought.

Sensing tension, his mother, as usual, stepped in. "Rick. You know your father takes an interest in you. He has a lot on his mind."

Rick didn't want to hear from his mother, though. He was tired of her excuses about his dad. He hadn't yet learned that he couldn't change his father. He would never feel the closeness he'd always yearned for. Throughout his life he would probably feel waves of sadness when he thought about this unleapable chasm.

Why was a relationship with his father so crucial to Rick?

Fathers—or father substitutes—serve an essential function during a growing person's separation phases. The first attachment figure is the mother. She's usually the first to hold the child while feeding. The quality of this early attention affects the growing child's sense of safety in the world.

The second figurehead, the father (or "other parent"), allows the child to become more separate from its mother. If the child knows there is another exciting person beyond its mother's arms, it is motivated to crawl away, explore, and trust the "broader world." This process of rotating between the familiar love of the mother and the exciting energies of the other parent (and the world beyond) repeats itself for many years. These shifts are crucial to the process of differentiation. For the boy child, a father's availability helps him to feel like a boy from the inside out. A father's hearty engagement in his son's explorations lead to the young child's robust engagement with life. This is why growing up without an interested father had become so troublesome for Rick.

If a parent is too distant and an adult child is in therapy, the offspring may try to reach the parent in new ways: sometimes through sending subtle notes or clippings and sometimes through a direct explanation of the problem or an angry confrontation. Instead of feeling pushed away like the too-close parent, the far-away parent may now feel drawn in, invited, demanded, and constantly reminded of the adult child's existence. This may make the parent feel confused and irritated. "What does Rick want?" "Can't he leave me alone?" "He's too old to act like this!" Although it's the son's or daughter's job to eventually grieve about what never was or will be, the parents can help themselves by being alert to these signs of yearning for parental involvement.

If adult children feel neglected by parents, their pain is so great that they usually avoid speaking directly about their desire for greater intimacy. After all, their greatest fear is being overlooked again! There may be sadness, avoidance, hurt, or anger in their eyes. The parents typically witness their child's pain when they show excitement about others instead of them. Watch for the hurt! Letting a spouse rescue the parent won't work. What the adult child wants is the parent's undivided attention. Turn off the television. Establish eye contact. Ask about current activities, thoughts, and feelings. The parent should convey that he or she is listening and remembering by referring to past conversations. Express admiration in specific, genuine ways!

Sybil

"So what is it, really, that you want from your mother, Sybil?" I asked her one day.

Sybil, an angry and bitter young scientist, had been so consumed with complaints about her too-busy mother that she had to stop and think. "I want her to take an interest in me. I want her to ask me about the people at work, and not about whether I've heard from my brother. Hmmmmmmm. I want her to notice what I'm embroidering—you know, really sit down and look at how tiny the stitches are and how complex the pattern is. I want her to praise me, but only if she really means it. I want her to stop talking about my old friends and all the children they have by now. I want her to ask about me." Sybil looked up. "Do you want me to keep listing what I want from Mom?"

I didn't reply.

"What do I want? I want her to be excited about who I am. I want her to smile. I want her to talk about me to me, and about her life and feelings, too. But Mom won't change. You get what you get in life. And me, I got a too-busy unhappy mom who can't sit down and smell the flowers."

With time and a number of indirectly bitter communications, Sybil began to tell her mother exactly what she longed for. Some wishes were based on deeply rooted memories of childhood deprivation and therefore could not be granted. With time, however, Sybil relinquished her dream of having a "perfect" mother. As Sybil refined her ability to state clearly what she wanted, she invested spurts of enthusiasm in her own ideas, projects, and friends.

From afar, I could tell that her mother was watching,

listening, and responding to most reasonable requests. Sybil's mother wasn't the overly personable sort, but she learned to sit down with Sybil. She learned to actually look at her daughter when they talked. She also began to talk about her own childhood, of her own loneliness and losses. When her mother began to share these things Sybil began to see why her mother always tried to preoccupy herself by staying busy.

In time, Sybil's pressing mother-hunger diminished. With restored energy, she reimmersed herself in the academic world. When I last heard from Sybil, she was travelling through Europe with her mother! On her postcard she scribbled:

"Having a great time. When I won the fellowship, I invited Mom to celebrate with me in France. We're making up for 'lost' time. She just loves the leisurely cafes of Paris (can you believe that?)—and so do I! Thought you'd be pleased. Love, Sybil."

I CAN'T CURE MY MOM

The Parenting Child

There are many types of "parenting children." In some ways, children are all invested in caring for their caretakers. Without them, how else could they have survived the helplessness of childhood? With well-nurtured parents, a child needs to do little more than be basically well-behaved, generally cooperative, and, with time, a competent and mutually loving adult.

If a child is lucky, its parents had enough of the "good stuff" (like love, self-discipline, and wisdom) to respond to its basic needs. If this was so, children's energies could be spent on learning, exploring, playing, and practicing social skills. Nevertheless, children have a vested interest in the well-being of parents. They may have tried, through excelling at sports or music, to enhance their parents' self-esteem by making them proud of them. When detecting parents' marital tensions, they may have distracted Mother and Dad by serving as anxious entertainers, funny peacemakers, or needy troublemakers. In subtle ways, children participate in keeping their parents emotionally healthy enough to provide for the children's safety and growth.

Some parents, however, were not fortunate enough when they were children to have healthy parent figures themselves. Raised in chaotic or depressed families or in homes where alcohol, physical, and/or sexual abuse prevailed, these parents' childhoods were either bleak or terrifying.

Emotionally deprived in childhood, these unnurtured adults enter parenthood without the reservoir of good feelings needed to enjoy and guide young children. For such parents raising children can be a depleting and exhaustingly unnatural act. When tired and emotionally overwhelmed, raising children becomes an endeavor of Herculean magnitude. It takes extraordinary stamina for emotionally impoverished adults to continue feeding, giving, clothing, training, and attending to the seemingly endless needs of children. With no internal nourishers to guide and comfort them, such parents often secretly wish they'd never had kids.

Still, these parents, unless they abandon their young, must endure the infinite demands of their children for many years.

"I felt like an empty pitcher," said an older woman of her child-rearing years. "I was constantly trying to pour out the milk. And even though you can't pour milk from an empty pitcher, I kept forcing myself to try. I would become angry and desperate. What I needed most was milk for *me*, but there was no place to go."

If, to some degree, parents feel that they had little nurturing as children they may have little to "give" as parents.

Their adult child doesn't know how hard it was for them to keep going. Nor is their adult child in therapy interested in the exertion required to raise his or her family. For the parent of this adult child their sorrows may seem even worse as they look after their offspring and think: All that hard work, and look how I messed up!

The enormity of such a parent's tasks combined with his or her vulnerability may be haunting, especially if the child is suffering because of the parent's limitations. If the parental struggles were severe, he or she may have repressed or forgotten those years (as well as the details of their own less than perfect childhood). Large, blank spots in memories often protect a person from the pain of past times. When memories fail, denial and "repression" (the tendency not to know, or to forget) are active. In certain cases children recall the details unless their memories are also too painful for review.

A child, in an effort to survive, probably did his or her best to make the parent happy if he or she was depressed. Kids may have cleaned the house, comforted a spouse, revived the parent if he or she drank too much, or avoided outbursts. To preserve the family's sanctity, children safeguarded family secrets at all costs. Sadly, despite a child's efforts to keep a parent functional, the mother or father may not have felt "parented." Their deficits and emptiness were too great. Nevertheless, the now-grown child may fit into the category of the "parenting child."

As a parent observes the struggles of an adult child in therapy he or she may conclude, "Despite my best efforts, I failed." This stabbing recognition hurts even though it is only partially accurate. Only the parent and not the child can know how arduous the task was. The adult child's fragility reminds the parent that his or her vulnerabilities prompted the child's suffering just as the mother's or father's own limitations may have fostered similar suffering.

Children raised by depressive, angry, abusive, or alcoholic parents may have developed special strengths and capabilities of which they are not yet aware. For example, parenting children may be exceptionally sensitive to the feelings of others. They unknowingly learned to be exquisitely attuned to every passing mood in the house. These "face scanners" watch the subtle changes and non-verbal cues of their friends (and therapists) with a highly trained eye. These adult children may be expert problem-solvers: the kinds of people who naturally know how to handle crises and emergencies. They are often considered "people-people." By contrast, some parenting children hid from the household chaos and applied themselves in extraordinary ways to reading and other mental pursuits. As adults they tend to be highly imaginative or intellectual.

Despite the capacities that parenting children developed in order to help the parent (and thus themselves) survive, parenting children may be emotionally depleted and internally fragile. Despite the strong armor they display to the world, some turn to alcohol, drugs, or other addictions to soothe agitation and depression.

But the parenting children of today have something that their parents probably didn't have: the assistance of skilled clinicians, support groups, and a psychologically minded culture to help them heal. If the parent is still suffering the jolts of his or her own youth, he or she can seek professional help, too. Although kids may be critical of the parent, parenting children tend to be fiercely loyal to their parents. This is why the separation process and leaving home is prolonged for many of them.

One problem shared by many of these adult children is a frightened inability to psychologically separate from their parents. As stated by a thirty-six-year-old man with whom I worked for three years:

"I woke up this morning shaking, feeling nervous, because I had this sudden realization that *I can't cure my dad.*

I can't make him give up alcohol. I've been trying all my life to cure my dad. Now that he's grown so thin, he looks like he's dying, which is scary. This morning, in my sleep, I guess it hit me: I can't cure my dad. While I'm trying to get healthier it seems he's getting sicker. Like he drinks more, smokes more, and gets angry more than ever. So then I wondered whether he's nastier than ever because I'm not there to cook for him any more. And the more I overcome my own problems, the less central Dad has become. Isn't that the way it *should* be. Like, isn't it natural for people to build a life for themselves?

"I wish Dad would join AA. It would be the greatest gift he could give me. I love him, but I can't cure him. It's frightening to want a healthy dad and to have found no way to cure him."

Turning his head to the side, Tom began to tremble. He wept like a terrified child until our session ended.

Parenting children fear growing up, because they dread the physical decline of their parents. In some cases, these fears are realistic. Often, when parenting children like Tom move out of their original households and direct their energies toward others, there are signs of declining health on the part of the parent. At this point, one can only hope that these parents, now left on their own, may seek professional assistance.

Parenting children, like most adults in therapy, often continue the separation process long after they have geographically left the household. Their struggle for inner confidence may continue, to the surprise of many, long after marriage.

"You'd think I'd stop having dreams about my parents now that I've been married for four years," said Ruth, an attractive costume designer of twenty-eight. "But last night I had almost the same dream I had last week. I was on an ocean liner headed to India. My parents were with me and we were having a good time; they looked so healthy and young.

Suddenly, the ship cracked in half—right down the middle! My end of the ship kept plowing through the water towards India but my parents' end of the boat just disappeared. It was terrible to see half of the ship, with my parents struggling, sink beneath the sea."

Sensing an incomplete thought, I asked Ruth whether that was the end of her dream.

"No," she responded almost apologetically. "My half-ship kept right on going. I landed in India, visiting new places and having a good time. So, what do you make of my dream?" asked Ruth.

I asked her the same question.

"It means I have this age-old fear that if I move on with life, my folks will sink. I also thinks it means I *want* to move on, despite these fears."

And that is exactly what Ruth did.

Do you think that your adult child in therapy is a parenting child? If you are now on a sinking ship or struggling in hidden ways, the best thing you can do for yourself and your extended family is to seek professional help.

One example is Serena.

Serena was a strikingly beautiful minister's wife. At age forty-eight she asked her adult son in therapy for the name of a therapist who knew about depression. Of course, she told Sam, she didn't want therapy, a friend of hers did. She held this name and number in her purse for two years while she thought remorsefully about all the "damage" she'd done to the people in her family.

Serena wasn't alcoholic and had not been physically violent. She had, however, had a hot, mean temper as well as a "nasty tongue" which would embarrass her husband, his parishioners, and her children. Her sons and daughter had often avoided sitting near her in the sanctuary. Back at home, they'd try to parent her by telling funny anecdotes and by remaining polite at all times.

Serena, like her own mother, was feisty only half the time. The other half of the time she spent in bed feeling dark, morose, paralyzed, and helpless. At these times her young children, especially her son Sam, would bring her tea.

Serena's mood swings were exacerbated whenever a family member left on a trip. When her minister husband Paul left town, her depressions turned suicidal. Eventually Paul was forced to refuse out of town commitments.

Serena's family members had encouraged her to seek help many times, but her response had always been: "Psychiatrists treat the crazy and I'm not crazy."

Two incidents finally motivated Serena to call the number she'd been carrying in her purse. First, she'd been looking through old scrapbooks of her children. On one yellowing page she saw a letter her daughter had written to her at the age of six.

Dear Mommy,

I'm sorry you're in bed again. Please get well soon. I feel so sad when you're sick. I like you better when you're happy. Please, Mommy, get well soon. When you get well, let's go to the movies and see Snow White.

Love,
Sally

In re-reading the letter, Serena could hear the pleas of her youngest child, the one who always brought her flowers. Then, to her horror, Serena thought about the story of Snow White, of the lonely little girl, of the wicked stepmother. Had she become the wicked mother? Serena searched her purse for the phone number. Then she folded up the paper again and went to bed.

The second motivator was her son Sam who, to her surprise, had grown increasingly gentle towards her while he was in therapy. His angry attacks on her "negligence" had disappeared. Once, when he stopped at the house to help fix the plumbing, he said, "Mom, therapy's not just for crazy folks. See, I'm not crazy. You don't have to be so miserable, but you must *decide* that you want to be happier if you want therapy to work."

"Want to be happier?" replied Serena from her couch. "Of course, I want to be happier."

"I don't think so, Mom," answered Sam. "You're *choosing* to be depressed. Otherwise, you'd be doing what you need to do." He bent over, kissed his mother's forehead, and went out the front door.

"So what do I need to do?" said Serena to the empty room.

She pulled the therapist's phone number from her purse for the last time. With trembling fingers, she dialed the number.

Within a year, and with the assistance of her therapist and medication, Serena became more active, consistent, and content than she'd been all her life.

"I just wish more people were aware," she told her therapist one day, "that you don't need to be crazy to get help. And you don't need to be young. But you do have to decide that you want to be happy. You should do it for your family. You should be happy for your children. Most of all, you should enjoy life for yourself. That's what life's for."

There are many ways to lead a fulfilling life. Psychotherapy is one of several routes that people choose to help with life's problems.

TRUE REJECTION AND THE FACE OF DEJECTION

"My parents were always loving—until they learned I was gay. I'm a concert pianist and my folks never missed a performance. They always invited me to play at their social events. Since I told them I'm gay, they've never invited me to their gatherings. They don't invite me for holidays. They don't call. It's hard to be the ideal son one day and an embarrassment the next. It's as if I'm not a person to my parents any more."

In a state of shock, Brett stared at me blankly through tired eyes. His friends had warned him that his parents might reject him, but Brett hadn't believed them. After all, his parents' best friends' son was gay. He'd always thought his folks were open-minded towards people different from themselves.

But when Brett had announced that he was gay, he was immediately ejected from the family circle. Feeling bitter, angry, and filled with painful dejection, Brett initiated therapy.

Ranges of Rejection

Although it may be difficult to imagine rejecting an adult child, some parents disinherit or even disown their children when differences become evident. Some parents, in shock, openly discredit their children for a whole range of reasons. They ask their sons or daughters to leave and never return.

In this section, I will not address the choices of parents whose children are violent. Serious problems often arise within families whose son or daughter departs from the expected cultural, marital, religious, or sexual family norm. These adult children are often loving, gentle, and unusually talented. They may be more emotionally stable than other family members. However, because of circumstance, preference, or personal orientation, they make noticeable choices that depart from those of their parents.

Interestingly, these young people's differences are often related to sexuality: sexual orientation, marriage, and procreation. Their lifestyle decisions trigger intense parental anxiety as well as fear of social disapproval.

A daughter, deeply in love, marries a man of great commitment but with a different racial background than her family. The parents, aghast, disinherit both of them.

An unmarried daughter becomes pregnant. Socially humiliated, the parents insist that she either seek an abortion or live elsewhere.

An unmarried daughter—a school teacher and writer—keeps her love life private from her parents. She secretly lives a thousand miles away from her family with a lesbian partner. When family gatherings occur, she travels home alone and is warmly welcomed. However, when she and her life-long companion adopt a child, Mary tells her parents the details of her private life. Her father, outraged, tells her never to set foot in his house again.

A white married couple with two blond sons adopts an Asian infant. After hearing about the interracial adoption, the wife's parents refuse to visit for holidays, to send gifts to the adopted child, or to speak with their daughter on the phone. Their previous pride in displaying photo albums is gone; these grandparents now hide their pictures and refuse to tell friends "what Tammy and Fred did."

Although many parents are flexible and enjoy their children's differences, therapists often hear stories about family cutoffs, evictions, and disownments. Intense parental hostility is often triggered by guilt, shame, and a prevailing need for social approval. When pride, religious ideals, or public position are threatened, such parents forget their deepest commitments. In an effort to hide their shame, they turn their offspring away from the family fold. The suffering of these parents is significant.

Nevertheless, I believe the pain, anger, and dejection of rejected children is far greater. If parents disinherit sons or daughters because they are "different," their adult children will legitimately question whether their parents loved them in the first place. They will challenge their parents' religious values and the motives of their parents' previous investment in them. They will struggle to continue believing in themselves despite the harshest of all repudiations: rejection by one's parents.

"I guess my parents could only love me as long as they could brag about me," said Brett, the pianist. "As long as they could show off my musical awards, my trophies, and photos, I was worth something to them. Maybe they only saw me as an appendage—as a way of making up for their own failures. Their love wasn't real love. I'm still me, with all the same talents and sensibilities that I ever had. The only difference is that they now know about one aspect of my life that they didn't know before. My folks overlooked the real me all along, I guess."

Brett was angry. He had lost his parents' support and affirmation. No one, he felt, could ever replace the appreciation he had once received from his parents.

Quite often people can't explain why they're so appalled by the circumstances of their children. They privately ask themselves questions like "Did we do something wrong?" Fortunately, many parents, after learning that a son or daughter is different than they are, educate themselves, readjust their expectations, and reach out lovingly again.

Our society, with all its variety and problems, offers new coping strategies for alienated parents and their offspring. For example, support groups for the parents of lesbians and gays help family members adjust to their child's revelation. Some parents grieve that they won't have biological grandchildren. Others must learn how to handle neighbors' insensitive questions.

There are few situations that someone has not found a way to overcome. It is within the parent's power to become better educated, find needed support, and reach out again to a rejected son or daughter. Adult children who have been rejected are usually powerless to rejoin the family if parents truly shut the door. They feel understandably bitter if their rightful place in the family is dishonored. They miss their parents' love.

If you are a parent who has shut the door on a son or daughter, you are also lonely, confused, and unhappy. Abandoning your adult child was the last thing you ever expected of yourself. If you need time to adjust to revelations from your child, you can tell your son or daughter exactly that: "This is really tough! I'll need time to get used to what you've just told me." Giving you time out is better than to be totally rejected. Most major cities offer resources for family members of people who choose other lifestyles. Consult the local mental health association, the local hotline, a social worker, or other mental health professional for information, so the lines of communication will be open to all your family members. This *is* within your power. The choice is yours.

CHAPTER 5

"TREAD SOFTLY," AND THE ANGRY DANCE OF LOVE

IMPERFECT LOVE

"My love for my wife is like a greeting card," said my client Mark one day. "Some people call my wife a saint."

"That's interesting," I respond. A greeting card."

"Sure," answered Mark. "My love for my wife is a greeting card; you know, the kind you send on Valentine's Day."

"You like greeting cards?" I asked casually.

"Well, actually, I have a hard time with greeting cards— most are a bit too unreal. They are just a bit *too* loving. Love's not quite that way. The cards are filled with love and sweetness and the things you don't *really* feel."

"So your love for your wife is like a greeting card?"

"Now I'm getting confused," replied Mark. "I think I'll start all over again."

People in therapy often want to believe that their love for their parents and loved ones is "pure." Not surprisingly, parents and loved ones like to feel "purely" loved. The fact, however, is that deeply loving relationships may be highly ambivalent. Affection may be tinted by sadness, annoyance, irritation, and an array of other emotions.

When children are young, parents usually feel deep love for them. Most spouses feel love for each other early in their marriage or partnership. Even that love, however, can be ambivalent at times. Why else do parents feel such love for infants—and even teenagers—when they're asleep? Parents love them when they're sleeping because their offspring's innocence and passivity bring forth tenderness. When babies are awake, no matter how much we love them, they make demands and often provoke their parents.

If parents and partners loved children and spouses purely, there would be no expressions like, "I'd like to wring his little neck," and no one would ever wish that they could "throw the baby out with the bath water." The mixed utterances of loving parents and partners attest to the fact that loved ones don't always feel tenderly towards the other person.

Why, then, do people expect the perfect love described by greeting cards?

When adults initiate therapy, one great fear is that the idealistic greeting card love may become damaged, ripped, or torn apart. Many people feel that anger is the opposite of love and dread reprisal. Even if people know such pure love can't exist, they fear its demise.

Outward responses to loved ones' therapies may be supportive. Indeed, interviews with parent groups and partner support groups indicate that many people verbally support the idea of therapy if they are sure their loved ones are working with skilled, ethical professionals. I have also found, however, that these same people often harbor private questions and doubts.

What will my loved one say about me?
I worry that I'll be misrepresented.

*Will the therapist try to make him mad at me for those
times when I . . .
I don't want him to hate me. I wasn't that bad.*

Many parents and loved ones, fearing retribution,
become skeptical about therapy and therapists when their children or partners start treatment.

"You're a therapist?" asked a good-looking man at a
recent dinner party.

I nodded. "Yes."

"Well, I better get out of *your* way," he said jokingly as
he swiftly glided to the other side of the room.

Because shame is such a painful emotional experience,
we avoid it at all costs. Everyone has delicate personal and
family issues which, if exposed, would result in great embarrassment. Most of all, however, parents and partners dread the
withdrawal of their loved one's loyalties. They also fear the
lessening of the other person's love—if they do hear angry
words, their greatest worry may appear confirmed: "You just
don't love me any more."

FRUSTRATIONS IN LOVE

As stated by Sheldon Roth, Harvard University psychiatrist and writer:

Common to all misery that enters the psychotherapist's office
is some frustration centered on love. It is love obtained and lost, love
sought, or love seemingly never found that disturbs people who seek
the attention and care of another person in defining a treatment for
their human ailment.

People don't come to therapists because they're angry.
They come because their love has been lost, injured, or

betrayed. People want to love. They want to like their bosses, enjoy their friends, and love their children, parents, and partners.

For this reason, when people initiate therapy, they are protective of their parents and partners, and the love they have for them. If they review frustrating, unhappy, or upsetting childhood events, they may feel some anger about those times. Many clients resist telling their loved ones about angry feelings, however. Like their parents or loved ones, many people in therapy are frightened of aggression—especially when it's their own. Adults unknowingly initiate therapy because they search for the healing of love's wounds.

Clinicians want to know whose love the client is seeking. They want to know how a person's capacity for love was thwarted. The initial link between a therapist and a client will be based on the early, affectionate images that the client retains from childhood. It was and is your child's trust in you, the parent, that allows new, constructive relationships to occur.

"Anger is an unhappy feeling," one of my youngest clients complained. "I don't want to be angry at anyone. Loving *feels* better."

ANGER IS UNHAPPINESS?

Anger is unhappiness because unhappiness lies under anger.

Indeed, anger emerges when one has been hurt, slighted, frightened, misunderstood, misrepresented, frustrated, ignored, violated, abandoned, or unloved. The list is endless. Therefore, when a client is angry, the therapist attempts to get to the "heart" of the matter. What injury inspired these irritated feelings? Who said what to hurt you? If anger is simply a cover for hurt, then why do so many people fear their own or others' anger?

Depending on which person you're talking to, the true answer varies.

Brendon

"You looked angry when I left my last session," an anxious young saxophonist proclaimed as he entered my office.

Not recalling any angry feelings, I said, "Really?"

"Yes, you looked angry and I think you were angry because I'd forgotten my dream. I hadn't meant to forget my dream, but I just forgot it. Next time I'll write it down."

Wanting to know more about this gentle man's experience of what he saw as anger, I inquired, "And what happened to you when you thought I was angry?"

"Well, for one thing, I thought it wasn't fair. I'm doing my best in here, but sometimes I just forget my dreams. So it wasn't fair of you to be so angry—not at all." Brendon was becoming agitated and spoke rapidly. "I don't think it's fair when people get mad when you've done a good job but forget one little thing . Just one little thing, like a dream, and poof, they're mad. It made me think of all those times when I was a kid and I would forget just one little thing. My mother would get so mad I was afraid to go home. Like the time I forgot to ask my teacher to give back my raincoat. I'd left it in the classroom and Mom said: 'Be sure you bring that raincoat home today!' But when school let out, I was with a gang of kids, and I forgot my raincoat again. I ran back to school to get it, but the school was locked. Boy, Mom sure will be mad, I thought. So I went to Joe's house and asked him, 'You know your old raincoat that looks like mine? Can I borrow it tonight?' But Joe had left his raincoat at Jim's house. So I thought, maybe I should find a way to get across town to Jim's. But I looked at my watch and it was six o'clock. Oh boy, I thought, I'm in deep trouble. I've forgotten my raincoat and I'm late.

"I got so scared that I called Mom from Joe's. 'Mom,' I said, 'I'm late because I'm doing homework at Joe's.' But Mom didn't believe me and started to shout: 'Your dad will be home in ten minutes and you better get here fast.' I can still hear the tension in her voice. I've never run so fast. I was scared of the dark but even more scared of Mom. When I rushed in the front door, I knew she'd be mad. I just hoped she might have forgotten about the raincoat.

"Well, it was quite a night. Mom came from the kitchen with that angry look. She held a big wooden spoon. 'You're late again, Brendon,' she almost yelled. I used to stand very far away when Mom got mad. You never knew when she'd smack you one or two in the face. 'And where's your raincoat?' she demanded.

"'The teacher lost it,' I said.

"'The teacher lost it? Since when do teachers lose raincoats?' It became one of those nights when I made sure to be very quiet and not say a word.

"You never knew when Mom would get angry. She never got angry at my brother Paul, so I decided she loved him more than she loved me. I decided I was especially bad. Sometimes she was loving and she'd forgive the worst things. But when she was mad, I couldn't sleep at night. I always worried about Mom getting mad. It might have been easier if she had gotten mad every time. At least I'd have known what to expect. The tension of it all made me nervous."

At this point, I commented that it must have been difficult for Brendon to attend today's session, given the fact that he'd concluded I was angry.

"You're right. I was awake all night just trying to decide whether to come. There was this voice in me that kept saying, 'Maybe Spencer wasn't all that mad, or maybe Spencer wasn't mad at all, or maybe she won't be mad by today.' So I decided to take the risk."

"So you didn't sleep all night?" I asked sympathetically.

"Only a few minutes. I had a terrible nightmare that woke me up."

"And I bet you forgot your nightmare!" I said with an affectionate chuckle.

"Sure did!" said Brendon. He started to laugh. He laughed so hard that he wept.

Brendon's connections with anger are uniquely his own. He associates "anger" with unfair punishment, unpredictability, and a "smack or two" in the face. To Brendon another person's anger means he's bad. Throughout childhood, Brendon made desperate attempts to avoid anger at all costs—even if he had to tell lies. He connects anger with forgetfulness, sleeplessness, darkness, and fear. When he gets angry he plays the saxophone. This way he knows that no one will get hurt. Brendon is only beginning to express his real feelings and protest that his mother's behavior towards him wasn't fair. He is tearfully grateful that I never get mad when he "forgets."

Some people are undaunted by anger. They grew up in families where anger was freely and clearly expressed. These were family groups that contained plenty of predictable love and in which the undercurrent of the family was consistently affectionate. There may even have been occasional swats on the fanny. But these well-intentioned swats were mixed with a good many hugs. These were families that didn't fear conflict because their conflicts were of the "safe" sort, like playful differences of opinion or flamboyant differences in style. People who can tolerate angry spats are generally people who don't fear violence or love's demise.

Sam

"My wife comes from a hot-blooded Italian family where

everyone screams and fights and loves each other," said Sam. "I'm different. In my family nobody got mad; although I think there was a lot of anger under the surface. That's why I get nervous when I see my wife starting to get mad. It never adds up to much, like 'Why the heck did you put your muddy shoes on the couch?' Comments like those make me very nervous. I have the religious viewpoint that anger isn't 'kindly.' I also have this fear that if someone gets mad, things could get out of control very quickly. That's why I want to run when my wife gets mad, which makes me feel ridiculous. She's half my size and never angry for long."

Sam, from a polite, religious, never-get-mad family, associates being angry with being unkindly. More significantly, he relates anger to "things getting out of control very quickly." There probably *was* a lot of pent-up rage "under the surface" in his home. Sam also has a problem differentiating between anger and other forms of aggression. Many innocent people share his naivete.

The following feelings may be perceived as anger: irritation, fatigue, boredom, disgust, dissatisfaction, vexation, displeasure, aggravation, hatred, complaint, or jealousy. Quite often, my clients report that their parents, partners and peers are angry when, in fact, their loved ones are simply preoccupied with their own thoughts or distracted.

Many people, interestingly, can't label this range of feelings in themselves. If they could, they would use these descriptive words more often to clearly communicate their grievances. I have noticed that clients prefer words like "irritation" or "annoyance" to "anger." This is probably because "anger" conveys, as defined by Webster, a "feeling of displeasure resulting from injury . . . and usually . . . a desire to fight back at the supposed cause of this feeling."

People who fear or prohibit angry dialogues tend to associate anger with violence, lack of control, and painful rejection.

Although religious doctrines often do discourage anger, people usually fear this feeling because it threatens their sense of safety or self-esteem.

If, as a parent or partner, you worry that your loved one may get angry at you for events of the past, please examine your use of this word. Also give thought to the source of your dread. Do you fear a dangerous fight? Or do you fear the withdrawal of your loved one's love just as you feared the loss of your mother's or father's affection? These are questions worth considering.

LOVE

Few of us worry about truly honest, loving relationships. Even if the love is imperfect, it is generally not a source of distress. When we feel loving, we are happy. Our faces light up and we smile. When we feel loved, we feel safe.

Self-confident adults accept themselves in indefinable ways. Although shaky or insecure at understandable times, the self-loving person is rarely troubled of mind. Rarely threatened by others' happiness or success, self-affirming adults freely give and receive affection.

Loving moments are described differently by different people because love includes so many shades and hues: affection, tenderness, admiration, peacefulness, romance, joy. When we care about someone in lasting and consistent ways, we feel at peace. Our actions are guided by a deep commitment to kindliness.

But when love is alternated with hostility, cruelty, dishonesty, impossible demands, or is judgmental, the recipients of this precarious love become anxious and confused. They may learn, for example, not to trust loving comments—never knowing when the next insult will occur.

Assumptions about love are infinitely variable. Whereas one person can give and receive affection without conflict, another may be tormented by hidden fears. Our brains actively store all memories and experiences. Both the people of our past, and our feelings in relationship to them, are retained in the unconscious. Thus new and current relationships will be viewed through mirrors of the past. This is why some people become so conflicted about love.

Jake

Jake was thirty-one when he initiated therapy. An unmarried biochemist, he lived with his widowed mother. Jake, while in his twenties, had led the wild life of the single "jock." All-night parties, motorcycles, pot, and sex offered exciting contrasts to his daily routines in the laboratory. At the same time, Jake felt obligated to his mother. He was her caretaker: sensitive, compliant, available, and practical. A pious woman, Mrs. Camelot was well known for her community work and her close relationship with Jake.

"What a fine son you have," the neighbors would comment enviously. "Imagine, having a son so loyal that he lives with you and takes you to church." Pleased, Jake's mother would smile proudly.

Jake had decided he would never marry. He enjoyed women, but there was one problem with them.

"Women are too needy," he said one day in my office. "I have yet to find a woman who doesn't grasp and cling and make me feel strangled. It's sad, because I'm very lonely. I lie in bed at night thinking, 'This loneliness is going to kill me.' So I tell myself, 'Get married, Jake. Just leave Mom. She can survive on her own; just get married.' Then, sure enough, on my next date, I begin to feel smothered, clutched at again. It's too bad, because love is supposed to feel so good. But to me, being loved feels like entrapment. When a woman says she loves me, I can't breathe. I want to push her away."

Jake was describing his conclusions about "love." As he began to look at these feelings and thoughts, he learned that his early relationship with his mother had been highly invested with nonverbal requirements. Although Mrs. Camelot had encouraged him to date girls in high school, she often grew depressed or anxious when he went out. In addition, his father, who had been chronically ill and died when Jake was twelve, had once implored: "If something happens to me, son, be sure to take good care of your mother."

Being a dutiful son, Jake had complied. Of course, his mother wanted Jake to marry. Yet a tape kept running through Jake's head that said: "Be a good boy. Take care of Mom." He grew to realize that he was often attracted to women who were needy of his care, just as his widowed Mom had once been. He also learned that his conflicted sense of duty to females blocked his capacity to love.

Thus Jake's frustrations with love related to his difficulty in feeling free in love. After realizing that he could love without feeling owned, he began to date women who were more self-sufficient and independently motivated and finally, he married. Afterward, Mrs. Camelot rented several rooms of her home to university students who admired her for her wisdom and caring spirit.

AGGRESSION

Jake needed *aggression* in order to pick himself up and find a woman of his own. By aggression I do *not* mean hostility, anger, or defiance, however.

Aggression is that force that supplies us the energy for separate, independent activities and motivates us to "get up and get going." Aggression allows young adults to move away from home. It takes aggression to apply ourselves to our studies, our talents, our job. This is not to say that aggression is separate from love. For example, a woman may both love her work and apply herself aggressively to the tasks of each assignment. A toddler's aggressive energy motivates her to crawl *away* from her mother to a toy across the room. A son's aggressive energy motivates him to search for that better job, or "Ms. Right."

For young adults to become emotionally separate from their parents, they need to access the aggression that will eventually propel them out the door. If you are a parent of an adult in therapy, you may notice that your son or daughter is becoming more aggressive. Sometimes his or her assertions will be subtle. At other times, these assertions may look like—or actually be—anger-propelled. But do not feel threatened. Young people *need* to tap the reservoirs within themselves that energize and activate the separation process.

Without healthy aggression, we might all be at home lying in bed. Although this might sound appealing for awhile, people who stay in bed all day are not happy. Dissatisfied with themselves, they watch life going by without them. They feel lethargic, unmotivated, apathetic, without energy. People who stay in bed all day have stymied the aggressive energy that not only says "time to get up" but also forces those tired legs to the floor and that sleepy head to an upright position. We need to access our aggression to do life's work.

Meagen

"I hope I'm not getting depressed again," said Meagen, an attractive artistic designer for the local museum. Meagen is tall with wavy brown hair. She always wears elegant classic suits. After years of trying not to "be gay," Meagen is now able to talk freely about her love relationships with women.

"I'd had a great week till Wednesday. Then yesterday I went to bed at eight o'clock. If I hadn't had this appointment, I'd have stayed in bed all day. I still feel tired after fifteen hours of sleep."

I could see from her puffy eyes that she'd been in bed a long time. I asked Meagen what might be roadblocking her liveliness.

"It's probably related to Jan. I can see she's attracted to someone else. She was sitting with Beth at the conference on Wednesday. I could tell they really liked each other. I felt so hurt. A dark, sinking feeling overwhelmed me. So, I left early, went home, and slept."

This is Meagen's typical pattern. When her love relationships are fulfilling, she is energetic. Her aggressive capacities find full expression in her art work. When her love is thwarted or threatened, her pain is so intense that she automatically loses her aggressive zeal and retires to bed.

Thus, we see a close relationship between feeling loved and being constructively aggressive in the broader world. Aggression and love feelings are intrinsically related. Children who feel securely loved and are encouraged with their activities are better able to access the aggressive energy needed to move away from home's comforts into their separate worlds of work and love.

For our purposes, we shall speak of aggression as that vital force that propels us to attend to our separate life tasks. When we are aggressively passionate—in our planning, our learning, and our work—we are thinking independently. Our minds are active on their own. Although we may be in the company of others, our aggression helps us to think creatively. Although inspired by interesting people and ideas, aggression is self-motivated. People who lack intellectual aggression cling to the ideas of others. Individuals who lack emotional aggression display compliance, submission, and passivity.

Aggression, like love, expresses itself in many derivative forms: determination, courage, motivation, assertiveness, energy, passion, creativity, and activity. People need to learn to access and utilize their aggression while maintaining meaningful relationships. Learning to channel aggressive energy cannot and should not be done in isolation. Our primary need is to stay in relationship. While "staying connected," we learn to act on our own.

It is important to focus on the concept of "aggression" because so many people misunderstand the early signs of healthy, robust aggressivity.

Diane

Diane was married two years ago. She is excited about her career as a paralegal, her five-month pregnancy, her new home, and her adoring husband. After years of depressive mood swings and anxiety attacks, she has become emotionally secure and relatively symptom-free. We have decided to discontinue her therapy after the birth of her baby. Diane wants to make sure she's in tiptop shape when her infant arrives.

Although Diane is internally insecure about her qualifications as a "grown-up" mother, she externalizes her conflicts, putting them onto something else. Instead of describing her *own* uncertainties, she obsesses over her mother's mixed feelings about her maternal capabilities.

"I don't know why," Diane whispers apologetically, "but I can't share all these feelings about the baby with Mom. I'd like to, but I wouldn't dare. I think this is why I've been getting stomach aches. It's always been this way. I feel sad, because I'd like to tell Mom about the toys we've bought, about the crib we refinished, and about our turning the guest room into a nursery. But, I think she wouldn't like all the excitement. She doubts that I'm ready to have a child. We were always so close," adds Diane. "I think she wants me to be her little girl forever."

Diane is expressing her own uncertainties about handling her multiple roles as a woman. She falsely concludes that her mother shares her concerns. Diane describes independent, assertive behaviors: refinishing a crib, redecorating a room, and preparing a nest for her family. But she thinks her mother distrusts her "readiness." Although engrossed in new activities, Diane subconsciously yearns to be her mother's little girl again. Her mother probably *will* feel both joy and melancholy when the baby is born, but her mother believes in Diane. Diane simply isn't ready to believe in herself.

Many parents subconsciously want their adult children to remain dependent children. Unlike Diane's mother, they discourage the healthy aggression required for adult living. Whether fantasized or real, the perception that parents don't want their children to "grow up" often precipitates angry aggression.

ANGRY AGGRESSION

One reason that aggression has such a bad reputation is that it is often equated with anger. Many people feel threatened by anger. Indeed, just as aggression propels the toddler towards the toy and away from its mother, aggression impels the adolescent to become a separate adult. If the parental environment truly supports individuality, young people may never display fierce or angry rebellions. However, if the young adult receives anxious messages that he or she is not capable of adulthood, a predictable tug of war ensues. In part, the war is between the actual parent and the young adult. But a greater battle is waged within those youths who are nervously proving their competencies to themselves.

Gene

"You asked me whether I'm *sure* that my parents resent my living in D.C. Of course I'm sure!"

Gene was angry at me for challenging him. He had been complaining that his parents resented his move to Washington, D.C. I was curious about whether his complaints were based on his own insecurities about living alone.

"You would know," ranted Gene, "how much they resent my living here if you could hear their phone messages! They're always calling me and leaving these sad messages. There's a reproachful tone in their voices if I'm out. What do they expect? For me to sit by my phone for their calls? I think that, because I'm the only unmarried son, they want me to be available. Like it's my obligation to care for them. It's my career and my personal commitments that they resent. When they ask if I'm coming home for the weekend and I can't go, there's always this long silence on the other end of the phone. I can't imagine taking a vacation without them. Can you imagine what they'd say if I took a trip to Hawaii by myself? I couldn't do that, they'd be so hurt. Now if I won a prize to Hawaii, that'd be okay, because I'd *have* to go. You know, it wouldn't be my own idea to leave them behind. I just don't think it's right. There shouldn't be this much conflict about having my own life. Maybe it's their loneliness that pressures me to spend time with them. I'm angry that they make me feel guilty about having a life of my own."

Gene paused to take a deep breath. "So, have I convinced you that my parents really resent my moving to D.C.?"

I give no response.

Gene, at age twenty-five, was very angry! Yet he chose not to express this anger to his parents. As he explored the meaning of his resentment, he learned that it served as a *distancer*, as a shield against his parents' actual hunger for him as well as his own insecurities.

When people feel loving, they are drawn towards each other. When people are aggressively angry, they act distantly.

Gene needed enough distance to practice living on his own.

Anger is a form of aggression, but aggression is often not angry.

"LOVE IS PATIENT, LOVE IS KIND . . ."

All great religions emphasize the importance of love, gentleness, kindness. Great leaders, writers, and religious visionaries remind us of the essential importance of loving ideals and behaviors. In a world so complex and vast, we are moved by the messages of spokespeople who help us to see ourselves and our world from expansive and hope-filled perspectives.

We're receptive to the loving worlds of priests, rabbis, and other religious leaders at times of birth, marriage, and death because we really want to be loving, honest, and caring. Yearning for harmony within our families and communities, we seek encouragement. We are at peace when the tasks of the day are done, knowing we've labored hard and are on good terms with the important people in our lives. These yearnings are universal.

Songs are sung about the peaceful places we have returned to in the past and still cherish. People are not inherently hateful, but some people have been hurt. This is why, in the absence of supportive intergenerational families, close communities, and wise elders, so many seek private places for their growth and pain. When conflicts overshadow the pleasures of loving, people turn to therapists, parents, partners, and peers for guidance.

If your loved one is seeing a therapist, he or she is both humble and resourceful. If, however, he or she becomes temporarily angry, contradictory, or distant, you may worry that long-held family values have been undermined. Such worries may not be necessary. When most adults complete therapy, they tend to be more mature, open, and compassionate towards their families that they were before. The basic values and religious ideas taught by their parents are more deeply appreciated than ever. As an adult child proceeds through the therapy process, he or she may become a better listener. The modeling of the attentive therapist has been valued and internalized.

If, instead of hearing love from your child, you hear hints of irritation or anger, please listen for the underlying message. When you are talking, you deserve to be heard. When your loved one communicates, try to listen for the meaning behind what is said without being jolted by the emotion. Constructive communication does not include name-calling or attacks on a person's character. Some people consider this abusive. Character-bashing blocks meaningful dialogue. Constructive communication requires talking about what *you* feel and think as opposed to what you presume *others* feel and think. Meaningful communication is built upon asking relevant, not merely provocative, questions.

Without clear, honest, and direct communication, family groups consistently fail themselves. Generation gaps are perpetuated. When people feel misunderstood they withdraw, feeling angry and hurt. As we try to communicate with our children and loved ones, we must use the correct words to convey our concerns. We must be steady. If we listen for the words and key messages that they are offering us, we will be regarded as attentive. If we are sensitive to their emotional truths, we will be rewarded by family and relationship harmony and deeper understanding.

Love is the work of attention.

Love is communicated through listening and speaking the truth.

Love is conveyed through understanding without retaliation.

CHAPTER 6

WHY
SO
VULNERABLE?

Whosoever loves much performs much and, can accomplish much, and what is done in love is well done!

Vincent Van Gogh

Dear Rachel,

Thanks for your letter. Of course, it was painful for your dad and me to learn that you're so unhappy and feel you had a troubled childhood. If that's true, it's the last thing we would ever have wanted for you. But, yes, everything you said made sense—except for one thing: if you think we didn't love you, then we must not have conveyed that love enough, or in the right way, because we loved you deeply. You were our first daughter: responsible, trustworthy, and helpful. Perhaps that was a difficult spot to be in, though. Did we ask too much of you? Maybe, some day, you'll begin to realize that, despite our oversights, you were a deeply loved child. I recall strolling you in the carriage—enjoying times all alone with you. You were such fun and funny. People would say, "What a precious little girl!" But something clearly went wrong if our love wasn't conveyed clearly enough. For that I am both sad and sorry.

As for your other comments, they all made sense. I think, once the other kids were born, you didn't get enough attention. My mom was sick. Do you remember Grandma Jane? She died when you were four. When she died, I wasn't the same person for a long time. And by then we had Jim, Bobby, and Sam. I can imagine you must have felt lonely and angry about being so displaced. I didn't have enough energy, and Dad's job wasn't secure. He was always worried about money. Our arguments—which you mentioned in your letter—were usually over how to pay the bills. I don't think I was as understanding towards your dad as I could have been. He was doing the best he could as a very young man. Actually, we were both only your age—twenty-six—by the time you were five! Did our disagreements scare you, or am I missing the point?

It's hard to grow old and look back at all the mistakes we made as parents—especially when we feel we hurt you so deeply. I'm glad you could tell us how you feel and that you're taking time to work these things through, as I know you will. You've always been good at solving problems..

If there's anything I can do to help you, let me know. I'm here.

Love,
Mom

This letter from Rachel's mother, Barbara, is constructive in many ways. Barbara doesn't deny that there were problems. She asks questions, trying to understand what her daughter is feeling. She legitimizes Rachel's anger and loneliness, and by saying she's "sorry," she claims partial responsibility for Rachel's distress. Barbara keeps the door open for communication. She refers to happy memories of being alone with her daughter; all children, regardless of age, cherish such references.

Barbara reassures Rachel that she's available, if needed, and states her confidence that her daughter can overcome problems. By not becoming defensive or displaying self-pity, Barbara conveys her strength. Open to the underlying message of her daughter's letter, she doesn't accuse Rachel of being unfair or ungrateful. Barbara's love is demonstrated by her effort to understand.

Nevertheless, Rachel's mother's letter couldn't heal the wounds of her lonely, fretful, resentful daughter; pretty Rachel had hoped for a letter from her father, too. However, her mother's empathetic letter set the stage for many future dialogues between her and her daughter.

Fortunately, this mother had been in therapy herself. By the time Barbara's own treatment was complete, she could love herself in spite of—and sometimes even because of—her own imperfections. This woman had a real advantage over many other people whose loved ones enter therapy. Therapy was neither mysterious nor threatening to her so she did not feel destroyed by the outraged letter Rachel had sent. A more vulnerable parent might have felt she had failed her child completely, which is never the case, or may have responded defensively and become hurtful.

NO AWARDS FOR PARENTING AND PARTNERING

As children, people become accustomed to receiving rewards for their efforts and accomplishments. Youngsters are applauded for their first words and steps, and exclamations like "good girl!" sing through the halls of supportive, happy homes. When children enter grade school, they receive stickers from their teachers and trophies from their coaches. Affirmed children grow to expect fair reward for their hard work. Children learn that if they complete a task to the best of their ability, they will be rewarded accordingly.

Recognition continues as a motivational force during the teenage years. Young adults are placed on the honor roll, honored at dinners, and given certificates of accomplishment. Those who enter the paid work force receive promotions, good evaluations, and a paycheck as proof and praise for a job assigned and completed.

But the hardest jobs of all, those of parenting one's

children, and partnering one's loved one, offer no tangible reward. This "awardlessness" is one of the problems today's adults, especially parents, wives, and husbands, struggle with unknowingly. Wives come to me saying, "I do everything for him. What's wrong?" Husbands say, "I'm busting my butt eighteen hours a day. Why does she complain?" Bright, dedicated parents who stay at home with young children often arrive at my office depressed and confused.

As stated by a sad, beleaguered mother of twins:

"I *chose* to stay home these years. I've always wanted kids. But I'm lonely; the jobs are endless. I clean, but the house is always a mess. The laundry never stops. It's so hard to be a mom. I want to go back to work."

On her first day of therapy, Paula wept and wept.

"You don't consider what you're doing to be *work*?" I asked.

"Of course, it's work. It's the hardest work I've every done. The problem is, no one ever says 'thank you.' I'm trying to teach my kids to say 'thank you, mama' but they sound like parrots. At least, at a job, you have a paycheck to show you've done something."

Paula, at twenty-nine, is as much of a perfectionist when it comes to the loving care of her children as she once had been with her pets, grades, hobbies, and career. However, now she is confronting the fact that the rewards of parenting are diffuse, unpredictable, and largely internal.

The enjoyment you feel pushing your child on a swing is a form of internal reward, but, before you know it, you're picking up your crying child from a mud puddle, hardly a gratifying experience. Furthermore, it may be difficult to take one's rewards from the simple pleasures especially for those who are goal-oriented. Parents today have trouble rewarding *themselves* for the enormity of their sacrifice and for their accomplishments as parents because they are accustomed to receiving external rewards.

Furthermore, they weren't prepared for the job!

Husbands, wives, and partners love each other, but aren't always prepared and don't always understand what is going to be demanded of them.

Regardless of one's age as a parent, everyone is an amateur at this "job." Children, of course, don't know that. Your children see you as strong, protective and loving, all-knowing, all-wise secure figures permanently in place in their lives. Sometimes, when adult children confront the fact that their parents weren't as perfect as they'd thought, they become disillusioned, but it's a healthy disillusionment because they, too, may one day become conscientiously imperfect parents.

Just as young parents, spouses, and partners must face the thanklessness of many necessary tasks, aging parents, spouses, and partners wrestle with the same challenge. Many parents, for instance, think, "by age twenty, she'll be on her way." Before you know it, though, not only Suzie, but Jeremy as well, is home for the summer—if not the year. Not only are they back in the nest, but now being verbal and potent, they challenge their parents differently:

"Why did you take the photos of Martin Luther King from your living room walls?" asked a socially concerned young grad student of his girlfriend, who had hoped he'd like her newly decorated studio apartment.

"Well, I wanted pictures of the peacefulness of nature in here," she responded.

"I'm afraid, Kelly," replied her significant other with grave concern, "that you're losing your values."

His girlfriend paused and murmured to herself: "Have I lost my values? My goodness, what has happened to my values?"

These loved ones confront who you are as a person. They are your spiritual watchdogs. Not only do they challenge your values, but also they confront you with who you are and who you have been as parents and partners.

"We're all spending the evening at Sally's," says college-age Jean.

"You'll all be at Sally's again?" bristles her dad. "Why don't your friends ever come to *our* house?"

"Well, you know," replies Jean with a softly hostile edge, "Sally's folks aren't as bothered as you are by the music and noise—plus they have a big family room, a ping pong table, and a new VCR."

Her dad looks at her mom, saying after their daughter leaves, "Are we that bad?"

No, of course, you aren't "that bad." Your partners and children meet others in the larger world. They're actively contrasting you, your family, and your values, with the new people they're meeting. They explore, compare, make decisions about their partners and parents. These comparisons, like the comparisons babies make between their fingers and your fingers, are essential for their individuation process. Hopefully, if your offspring have absorbed your attempts to teach them to be considerate, they will show some compassion. If you have been considerate, your partners will be also. Even so, their true impressions often leak out unexpectedly.

Sometimes partners and adult children display great pride when they bring home their friends to introduce to their parents. At other times, they blush with embarrassment.

"My mom's eyes aren't usually that puffy," a daughter whispered to her friends after her forty-year-old mother left the kitchen.

Are my eyes puffy? thought her mother as she overheard their whispers.

She headed for the bathroom mirror: Good grief, do I ever have droopy, puffy eyes! I'm getting old . . . I'm getting old. She disappeared to the bedroom and felt sad.

WHAT ADULT CHILDREN DON'T KNOW

As many things as sons and daughters may be challenging, there's a lot they don't know about their parents. There's a lot they don't know about life, supporting a family, parenting, and aging. In particular, despite their brilliance, they don't know who you really are! Personal backgrounds are complex and, at this point, far more variegated than their own. Your children may never meet your parents, your grandparents or the people and places from your pasts. In some ways your children know who you are to the core, but in other ways, there will always be a mysterious chasm between who you are and how your children perceive you. Enduring this time warp is part of being a parent.

Your offspring can't truly grasp that when their parents were young, they also led a separate life of their own. Children—unlike anyone else—see their parents in one fixed role: parent. Their ignorance about who the parent really is protects them from the parent's terrifying fallibility. Young children need to see their parents as being one hundred percent parent. This perception provides them with a sense of safety.

Children see parents as the face that joyfully applauded their art work, choral concerts, and basketball games. They catered the birthday parties, took the pictures, and made the scrapbooks. Kids counted on parents for hot dog roasts and picnics in the park. Almost all that they enjoyed was provided by the hard work and determined energy of their mothers and fathers.

While these good times will be remembered by everyone with pleasure, children can never really understand that their parents also had impelling private concerns which had nothing to do with the children. Sometimes these other things were the routine challenges of living: paying for the car, dealing with the landlord, or smoothing out misunderstandings with elders.

However, many parents faced horrendous hurdles while raising their children. Although they protected their children from these private catastrophes, their kids' lives were nevertheless influenced by their parents' crises. Keenly equipped with emotional antennae, these now-adult children see therapists in order to recover from the distress they absorbed but could not understand. Many aging parents, whose adult children are now in therapy, faced big problems.

I will share with you some facts about the parents of several confused people who are now in therapy. These clients feel "in the dark" about facts they were never told. Befuddled and lacking self-esteem, these clients can only fantasize about what "went wrong." They feel chronically defective in profound and perplexing ways:

Jane's parents almost got divorced after the death of their first-born infant, about whom Jane does not yet know. Jane was considered "second best" by her parents and was held in the arms of a grieving mother. Her parents' distress was inconsolable. Jane has concluded that she always feels "second hand" and "second best" because she is "ugly."

Mike's mom had not wanted to have children, but his dad had insisted. "Mom always smiles and 'acts' loving," states Mike, but he can't *feel* her affection. He wears a chronically forced grin, just like his mom's, but doesn't know why.

Patty's dad was fired from his job and was clinically depressed at the time she was born. It wasn't until the birth of her parents' third child that his dad was on his feet and back on the job again. Patty can't understand why she's so fragile whereas her brother and sister are emotionally robust. She's decided she had "bad genes."

Pamela jumps when people approach her physically. She doesn't know that her dad used to hit her just as hard as his mother hit him. Despite her dad's efforts to contain his rage, he had struck out only at Pam—who resembled his mother. Pamela figures that Dad hated her because of something "bad" deep within her. She can't decide what her "flaw" is, but is consumed by self-hatred.

Becky doesn't know that when she was young, her mother was struggling with a drinking problem. Her mother's recovery was riddled with blackouts, slips, and despair. Although her mom became a hero in her own right, Becky doesn't understand why she can't tolerate seeing her mother unhappy. She fears leaving her mom's side and has decided she is "fated" for spinsterhood.

Lila has a vague sense that life was once "sunny and fun." For some reason, life turned dark—when she was four or five? What she doesn't know is that after her grandmother died, her mother lost her "love of life." Lila believes that she "lost" something. In her dreams she knocks on doors—as if searching for someone. "Do you think I was adopted?" she asks.

Mickey doesn't know that her mom and dad—who had each been raised in foster homes—didn't know much about parenting. His parents feel ashamed of their orphaned backgrounds and don't want to tell Mickey about their childhoods. Mickey has "weird" fantasies that his grandparents were murderers.

All parents have lists of gripping, real life crises which influenced or coincided with their parenting years. Although happiness may have also marked their lives, celebrations rarely interfered with enthusiastic parenting. Parental zest is always hampered by personally draining, conflictual "hard times." In attempting to protect your children from your personal crises, you may not have complained, but those "mysterious" challenges which you valiantly endured affected your children, despite your best intentions. Fights with your spouse. Crying spells. Job loss. The death of a friend. Emotional exhaustion. All affect children. "Mommy's sad because I've been bad" is a common interpretation by a child.

Adult children have difficulty grasping that people happen to be parents instead of that parents just "happen" to be people. Since you are the only ones who battled your personal crises while parenting, you are the only ones who can offer yourselves true compassion. Therefore, you must be respectful of yourselves when children attack because of problems they do not understand that were out of your control. You must be your own inner peacemakers if your children challenge you about hard times. The more you can be compassionate toward yourselves, the more sensitive you will be to the emotional sufferings of your adult children.

By fortifying yourselves with self-compassion, you prepare for your adult children's homecomings.

THE TRUTH COMES HOME

Animated with new ideas from their adventures in the world, young people inspire older ones and keep these older minds flexible. If they are excited about their voyages, their parents' world becomes wider, too. History has relied on the insights, protests, and visions of young adults. Because of their freedom and fresh perspectives, young people see what needs to be changed. They challenge injustice. The powerful energy that propels youth is sometimes contagious. It is often brilliant—and delightfully grandiose.

Sons and daughters need this grandiose vision to give them the courage to define who they can become. Yet they, like their parents, see only partial truths.

Listening to adult children speak of their early years, one must remember that they are speaking their truths from *their* perspectives. Young people's emotional truths are of crucial importance to them. Their growing-up years were so recent that their memories are vividly replete.

When young people tell parents of their hard times as children, they press their parents to make up for lost time. Back then, their parents may have been too busy to stop and really listen. They may have been too distracted—for reasons they still do not understand—to attend fully to their children's needs. Furthermore, small children may have been too young to artic- ulate all they felt.

If young people can speak their truths openly now, their parents must give them undivided attention. They must listen and speak honestly, even when the truth hurts.

Claire, a woman of fifty, told me the following story:

"I'm so glad I had completed therapy before Mom died. I'd been such an angry child, and Mother died young. We'd fought like cats throughout my youth. She was often selfish. In the presence of my sisters she was openly rejecting of me.

"While I was in therapy, we started talking together. She finally admitted that I had always reminded her of her father— who had been cruel to her—because of my dark complexion. She'd always felt guilty about her treatment of me. By the time she died, we'd made peace with each other. I grew to appreci- ate her high-spiritedness, her wit, and her humor. After our long conversations about what had obviously gone wrong for me, our affection deepened. We expressed our feelings openly.

During her failing years, I was her most attentive and religious daughter. I'm glad we could talk before she died. I'm glad she could admit the truth. Without the help of my therapist, I'd never have been able to tell my mother I loved her. I would never have believed that she loved me."

BARRY'S WIFE, MOTHER, AND "WORKING THROUGH"

"My husband is working through some angry times," said Barry's wife to her friend. "He's angry towards his mother, his dad and me. He was in a rage last night. It was terrible! But at least he's talking."

"Working through"—a clinical term—refers to emotionally reliving a past experience in order to make sense of it. It is a common psychotherapeutic expression, because people in therapy attempt to review and then make sense of past experiences.

We are all working through issues without knowing it. If you're remembering the feelings you had on the elevator when you overheard your boss talking about you, you're working it through. "Mulling it over," "trying to figure it out," and "dealing with it" are popular terms for a similar process. When a person is working through what happened yesterday, he or she continues the feelings of that moment with relevant thoughts. A term related to "working through" is "processing." When we process new ideas, we're trying to organize, internalize, and reshape thoughts for useful purposes. You need to know these terms because your adult children in therapy will probably use them.

When people work through a past experience, they relive the feelings as well as the thoughts related to that event. For this reason, when Barry's wife said her husband was "working through some angry times," she meant that Barry was feeling some anger and rethinking past events. The wife revealed to the therapist that Barry was "reworking" the day his dad had walked out. Along with fear, Barry had felt angry and confused. He was only five when his father left. His mother, in tears over her own hurt, was in no position to listen to Barry's pain.

Therefore, five year-old-Barry had survived his father's abandonment by retreating to his room, not causing trouble, and acting in a loving manner to his tearful mother. Now, years later, Barry's parents have remarried. But Barry is reworking emotional memories so they won't resurface in his own marriage. Last night at dinner, Barry's anger was charged with biting accusations.

Lynn, Barry's mother, doesn't want to be reminded of those difficult times. Tim, Barry's father, feeling misunderstood, doesn't want to look back either. Their mutual guilt and despair have diminished with the years. They've had time to discuss their misunderstandings, to forgive and forget. But Barry hasn't forgiven his parents, nor has he forgotten.

His wife, not having been there, does her best to understand, but doesn't completely. In my experience, true forgiveness occurs when people have had the opportunity to grieve, understand, and heal after an injurious life crisis. With time and effort, many—but certainly not all—"unforgivable" situations can be made genuinely "forgivable." A lot depends on the extent of the damage and the eventual degree of recovery.

"A worrisome fact," said Lynn to her own therapist, "is that Barry doesn't know why his dad walked out. Last night he began asking, again, what really happened when he was five. I grew very nervous. I don't want Barry to know that we'd both had affairs. I don't want him to know that I'd had an affair, too. After all, he doesn't know why we *both* had affairs."

"So he *does* know you both had affairs but he doesn't know why?" her therapist inquired, puzzled.

"Now I'm getting confused," said Lynn with irritation. "Well, sometimes I have this feeling that Barry has figured it out . . . that he kind of knows, you know."

"Yes," agreed her therapist. "Family secrets are usually 'known.' That's why they're troublesome, the knowing, but not knowing enough."

HOW MUCH SHOULD PARENTS TELL CHILDREN?

If adult children ask questions about situations in their childhoods that were private to their parents, should you answer their questions? If so, how much should you say?

There is no simple answer. If a parent is truly perplexed about whether, or how much, to answer the adult child's questions, speak with a professional before responding. The parent can always say, "That's an important question, but I'll need time to think about it." The following guidelines for answering personal questions may be helpful.

First, the truth is better than confusion. If people are confused, they create fantasies to explain what they can't understand. Usually their fantasies are far more personalized, frightening, and debilitating than the actual truth. When essential facts are missing, people tend to blame and shame themselves. This is why telling the truth—even when painful—is an important guideline when responding to questions. Do not forget that children are intensely repulsed by hypocrisy!

Barry is confused and angry that his Dad walked out on the family. Dad has been implicated as the sole abandoner. Had Dad walked out because he was tired of Barry? Didn't Dad care about his role as a father? Barry doesn't want to think of his dad as the "bad guy," but he doesn't understand. He definitely wonders whether he'll do the same to *his* wife.

Second, like the adult child, a parent or partner has the right and need for a "private self." Some boundaries—for everyone's sake—should be maintained.

Lynn, Barry's mother, doesn't want to speak explicitly about her affairs or sexuality. She feels that those events were hers alone and private. There are ways she can respond honestly to Barry's questions without betraying her own sense of privacy.

Third, the answers a person is seeking should relate to problems that are currently confusing or bothersome. The parent or partner doesn't need to tell every detail or his or her entire life story.

Barry seems to know that his dad wasn't solely responsible, because his mom becomes angrily defensive when the old family crisis is discussed. Yet his father was the one who walked out. It might help Barry to know that his parents had had some grave misunderstandings and were too depleted to support each other that year. They were equally responsible for Barry's dad's decision to leave. They had both made serious mistakes and needed time apart. They love each other now, and such a crisis will not occur again.

Fourth, the information an adult child seeks is determined by the child's unique reactions to the crisis.

Barry has always tended to be overly protective of his wife. He annoys her when she is upset by trying to rescue her (as he tried to rescue his mother years ago). He also lives with fear that, like his father, he will walk out in a rage on his wife. With a clearer picture of the mutuality of his parents' marital crisis, Barry will be able to make sense of—and correct—his own irritating behaviors and fears.

Fifth, if the parent or partner wants to share painful information, he or she must be prepared for an emotional response. Although the needed information may calm an adult child eventually, the parent cannot count on this.

For example, if Barry learns that his mother was equally responsible for his father's departure and wasn't just an innocent victim, he may decide he'd been duped and exploited. He may feel new compassion for his father who had carried the onus for so long. However, on some level, Barry always knew the truth. He will grow to appreciate his mother's honesty, because she was courageous enough to clarify the issue *for his sake*.

Sixth, clear, simple explanations are better than long-winded ones. The parent's or partner's personal honesty and concern for the loved one's well-being are aids to healing.

Barry doesn't need to know all the details about his mother's or his father's affairs or the personal problems that prompted them. He needs simple, *honest* answers that relate to his specific questions and concerns.

Seventh, old crises can be repeated if the facts aren't shared in a personally responsible manner. Partners and parents harm their relationships by blaming the loved one for problems that were—or are—of their own making.

If Barry begins to ask questions about what *really* happened when "Dad walked out," his parents will recreate the crisis if they respond to his questions angrily and accusingly. Some parents might want to avoid the topic by saying, "Barry, why do you always cause trouble by bringing up this topic again and again? You know how painful it was for us, and we're getting upset all over again!" By responding in this way, the parents might once again make Barry feel hopeless, angry, and at fault. If Barry's parents have his best interests in mind, they will quietly respond that although the topic is upsetting to them, they will discuss it because he deserves to understand what happened. After all, the event was more confusing for him than it was for them.

Eighth, when speaking honestly about personal mistakes or failures, parents and partners can expect to feel vulnerable, embarrassed, and exposed.

Sometime in the future, when Barry makes mistakes or disappoints himself, he will be able to turn to his partner or his parents for guidance. He will know that even they made mistakes, but can speak the truth about them even if it hurts. Even if it's embarrassing. Even if it's shameful.

THE REASONS LOVED ONES FEEL VULNERABLE

There are many reasons why loved ones feel vulnerable in relationship to their partners. Without question, thousands of fortunate people, including parents and children, enjoy mutually affectionate relationships with each other. For these, the growing up years were relatively untroubled by emotional disharmony, physical abuse, marital conflict, mental illness, or other major stressors. Having been constitutionally strong and well-enough nurtured during their own childhoods, these people become parents and partners who shower affection and wisdom on their loved ones. These families are fortunate.

However, even in fortunate "functional" families, surprising things happen. A son may announce that he's gay. A daughter may do the same. A child, for reasons that are yet unclear, may display early signs of severe mental illness. A spouse or partner may do the same. Young adults may move so far away that the cost of yearly visits home becomes prohibitive. A previously accomplished husband may be arrested for drug use, and a "happily married" daughter may announce a divorce. No adult relationship is immune from the ongoing surprises and crises of life. At these times, responsible, caring parents and partners wonder: "Did we do something wrong? How can we help?" Their questions, along with the sadness they feel when their loved ones are suffering, leave them vulnerable.

If a parent or partner can tolerate feeling imperfect, partially responsible, sad, or temporarily rejected, these vulnerable times may be used constructively. However, if the person's self-esteem is delicate or personal liabilities make normal living painful, the parent or partner may be what I call "exquisitely vulnerable."

124

Exquisite Vulnerability

"Exquisitely vulnerable" parents are especially fragile because they can't tolerate their human frailties. Lacking resilient self-esteem, they are easily injured. Insecure about their personal worth, these vulnerable parents often depend for their happiness on their children's admiration and public success. Thus, when children fail to meet these parents' needs or expectations, exquisitely vulnerable parents feel shamed, angered, or emotionally threatened. Exceptionally invested in the lives of their children, they feel defiant or devalued when their sons and daughters fail.

These vulnerable parents are unusually sensitive to the critiques of their children. When challenged, they often lash out at their offspring through anger, blame, or self-pity.

If ever there is a time when parents are scrutinized as people and parents, it is when their children are young adults. This parental scrutiny feels especially unnerving if an adult child is having emotional problems and is speaking with a therapist. When parents protest, they find to their horror that they only complicate their tenuous relationships with their offspring. "Are you saying that I'm at fault?" "What are you saying about me to that therapist?" "How ungrateful can you get?"

Whether or not parents consider themselves to be "exquisitely vulnerable," the aging process further magnifies self-doubt.

The Aging Process and Self Review

People inevitably grow older. If their children have left the house, parents may feel more alone than ever before. Spouses or parents may be ill or dying. They may look back on their most vital years with both satisfaction and regret. Despite new activities, they are in a period of major transition. Yet, the transitions of their young adult children appear more urgent than their own. "But of course," they claim heroically, "life is difficult out there. The children are young! Parents already know how to live, but the children are just learning."

But we are *all* in transition. Many of us don't give adequate attention to the process of self-review, even when we're absorbed in it. Some older adults feel private about aging. Unwilling to burden our children with philosophical questions about life, we deprive our youth of evolving spiritual maturity. America's aging population is only beginning to receive the dignified respect it deserves. In many cultures, older people automatically assume new and respected social roles. This is rarely the case in America. Growing middle-aged and older—like "growing up"—is a complex task. Parents carry their own share of grandiosity about what is happening to them. "Oh, this arthritis is really nothing!" "I'm too old to get upset about such things," they say, disguising their concerns.

As stated by a dignified professor of eighty, "I'm just too vigorous to move to a retirement community. I'll wait until I'm eighty-five." By the time he was eighty-four, he was "too old" to be admitted to the community of his choice.

Judith Viorst in, *Necessary Losses*, says, "The task of a development transition is to terminate a time in one's life; to accept the losses the termination entails; to review and evaluate the past . . . and to consider one's wishes and possibilities for the future . . ."

Thus, at the same time that parents are performing their own "life reviews," whether they are in their forties, fifties, or seventies, adult children in therapy approach them with their own reviews. If they enjoy remembering the happy trips, the family celebrations, and the good times of youth, the parents feel rewarded. However, if adult children are struggling emotionally and need to "rework" childhood grievances with parents, the parents usually feel unappreciated.

"It hardly seems fair," said Denise, a woman of sixty. In therapy she's been reviewing her life as a fatherless child, a husbandless mother, and the sole survivor of her sibling constellation. "Just as I put the hard times behind me, in pops my son Jeremy to remind me of them again. I'm ready to live in the present, but he's not."

Unfortunately, Denise carries the full weight of Jeremy's pain instead of simply listening to it. Despite all her talents as a flower shop manager, Denise is a fearful parent. She has difficulty balancing active concern with the capacity to distance herself from others' problems. She feels she must become involved with, if not in control of, Jeremy's life. Unable to trust that her son can find solutions of his own, she displays a life-long pattern of self-blame.

Self-Blame Versus Self-Love

As much as parents or partners want to be honest, supportive, and available to their loved ones, they do not need to make all their children's or spouse's problems their own. Many of the issues that challenge loved ones are *not* of the other person's making. Adults enter therapy for many reasons. They seek the support of therapists because they are lonely or believe they are not perfect enough. They need outside support because their relationships feel shallow or they face too many choices. In our psychologically minded culture, parents and partners often assume too much guilt, too much responsibility, and too much pain for problems that either are—or are not—of their own making.

Parents and partners do not help their children and loved ones by claiming total responsibility or blame for the many problems that challenge the other person. Parents and partners help no one by becoming self-reproachful or pathologically guilty. By enhancing their communication styles, parents and spouses become more capable of listening non-defensively and speaking the truth. Parents and spouses must convey trust that their children and loved ones can—and will—overcome their life challenges just as *they* have done. Adults convey strength by demonstrating personal courage, honesty, and self-respect. Parents who are emotionally genuine become models of dignity to younger generations. We owe ourselves the right to live and age with integrity.

TOO LITTLE LAUGHTER

Each day, and the living of it, has to be a conscious creation in which discipline and order are relieved with some play and pure foolishness.

May Sarton

Any parent or partner who has taken the time to read this book is, by definition, "serious-minded." You wouldn't be reading this lengthy "letter" if you took parenting, your adult child's well-being, or the quality of your relationships lightly. Many parents and partners, because of their seriousness, laugh too little. They are totally accustomed to watching for problems and finding solutions.

However, the solution to a too-little-laughter problem is not simple. We all know that merriment is good for the soul and our health. Some of us do little to *create* mirth. The more people can create merriment—through watching funny films, by telling humorous anecdotes, and by acknowledging the innumerable ridiculous situations that surround them—the healthier families will become. Young children respond instantaneously to the funny touches of life. Have partners suppressed this capacity for joy because life has truly been so hard? Have loved ones become so serious that they have *forgotten* how to laugh?

Although no one can find humor in truly tragic times, parents and partners of those in therapy often deprive themselves of tragedy's antidote: the ability to laugh. Laughter is a way of showing love. Delight and loving laughter convey that not all has been lost. Laughter emphasizes the aliveness of our spirits. It reinforces *life*.

Although there is no one prescription for mirth, may I recommend that parents and partners play with the possibility of putting more merriment into their lives?

CHAPTER 7

"HOW
CAN
I
HELP?"

*If you have made mistakes . . . there is always a chance for you.
. . . You may have a fresh start any moment you choose, for this
thing we call "failure" is not the falling down, but the staying
down.*

Mary Pickford

THE LADY WITH THE CARE PACKAGE

Rosanne, age thirty-seven, drives ninety-five miles each
Saturday to visit her widowed mother. Each Saturday, her sev-
enty-year-old mother, Edith Rosenberg, waits by her window
and welcomes her daughter with hugs and gentle kisses. A
stooped, soft-eyed woman who wears bright sweaters, Edith
always presents Rosanne with a basket of homemade sweets:
delicate macaroons, fig bars, and tart sugar cookies. Mrs.
Rosenberg uses a walker to move through her small kitchen.

One week, Edith became ill. Her arthritis grew so severe
that she couldn't open the door. Nevertheless, she baked her
typical assortment of unusual sweets for Rosanne.

Arriving at the small apartment, Rosanne grew alarmed about her mother's health. When her mother presented her with the doily-lined basket of pastries, Rosanne exclaimed: "Mother! You shouldn't have gotten out of bed to do all this baking! Why must you always make these baskets?"

Mother and daughter sat side by side on the drab couch. Edith began to weep. "I want to make up for lost time," she whispered through her tears. "I want to make up for all I couldn't give you when you were little."

"Make up for what?" asked Rosanne, who, as an uncomplaining child, had been flagrantly overlooked by her clinically depressed mother who worked with her husband in a busy shop. Rosanne's adulthood had been consumed by depressive loneliness and, eventually, psychotherapy.

"You know too well," wept Edith. "I was overwhelmed . . . depressed, when you were small. Running Dad's shop took all my energy. I know I didn't give you the attention you needed. I'm so sorry." Mrs. Rosenberg's frail body doubled over.

She and Rosanne held each other.

"You were a good mother," wept Rosanne. "You did the best you could."

"But I *am* sorry," Edith repeated. "These baskets are the only way I know to give you what I couldn't give you then."

Rosanne and her mother wept, holding each other, until the pain subsided.

HOW CAN I HELP?

"Is there anything I can do to help?" ask parents and partners of people in therapy. "How can I help?" "Should I help?" "What can I do?"

There are several answers. The most important answer is that it is never too late to "begin anew" to enrich family or relationship ties. This means, of course, that a partner or parent can become increasingly respectful of an adult child's independence and strengths. If children or loved ones are in therapy, that therapy is just one aspect of their busy lives. By becoming more educated about mental functioning, adult development, and the therapy process, the parent or partner has already begun anew. When things happen, the parent will be prepared. If a parent or spouse is becoming more honest with himself or herself, and is more inwardly accepting and more resilient to criticism, he or she is beginning anew. And, perhaps, this will bring some laughter back into the other person's life. By moving ahead with the opportunities of his or her own freedom, the loved one of the person in therapy will find his or her focus re-energized. The partner is setting the stage for the years ahead when he or she and the loved one can relate more enjoyably.

In a society where loneliness attacks all age groups, the value of the realigned, ever-expanding family network must not be minimized. Changes occur rapidly in this complicated world. It is never too late to create safe havens for our children and to enhance our capacities for loving relationships.

"How can I help my husband with his therapy?" asks Ann Holder.

Perhaps I haven't been clear. The process called "therapy" is your loved one's business. Your "business" is to find more constructive, accepting, and authentic ways for relating to your partner or child.

Individual therapy is private, self-directed, and disciplined. The partner or parent may not be invited to "help." Adult children or partners in therapy are taking care of their own lives. They are keeping afloat in new ways. Swimming valiantly into adult life, their own capacities keep them from drowning.

At the outset of his therapy, Jim, a young athlete, reported recurrent dreams of being cruelly thrown into the water although he did not know how to swim. He would struggle against the water, sinking, choking, and gasping for breath. As his therapy progressed and he acquired a new sense of competence, his dreams revealed that he had become an Olympic swimmer who could not only dive into the water but also win the race. Jim had become master of his own life.

DIFFERENT CLIENTS—DIFFERENT PARENTS AND PARTNERS

Although a parent or partner may not be invited to join in a loved one's therapy session, he or she may be curious about relationship or family issues that are commonly referred to during therapy hours. Let's look at several types of parent-child and partner patterns with which people in therapy often struggle. Can you see yourself in any of the following vignettes?

The Supportive, Non-Intrusive Parent and Partner

Many clients know their loved ones support the treatment process. Their parents or partners are available to help them if called upon. Respectful of their adult children's or spouse's boundaries, these parents and partners rarely pry or ask intrusive questions. They convey respect by trusting that their loved ones are resourceful enough to solve their private problems.

Randy, the twentyish son of a non-intrusive mother once commented, "Last night, I told Mom that my therapist is pretty amazing. I said, 'Mom, this therapist is pretty cool. She says I'm a late bloomer.'

"Mom went on rinsing the dishes and said, 'I'm so glad you like your therapist, Randy.' That's all she said. Mom's cool. Don't you think my Mom is cool?"

Randy was pleased that his mother could respect him without asking too much, without prying, and without feeling threatened by his relationship with a therapist. She could rejoice with him that he was growing to like and trust his therapist. Her acceptance facilitated Randy's appreciation of his mother.

A husband, whom I interviewed for this book, said the following:

"Since Jan's been in therapy, we've been confiding in each other more. There's a lot more openness between us. But one thing I never ask about is her therapy. If she wants to bring it up, fine. I *never* ask what happens in sessions, or what she's 'working on.' There are many things Jan and I talk about these days, but—despite my curiosity—one thing I never ask about is her therapy."

Though most adults tell their partners, many never tell their parents about being in therapy. Preferring independence and privacy, these clients don't need to discuss this undertaking with their folks. "After all," stated a young salesman, "I'm in therapy for *me*. There's no reason to involve my folks. It feels great to be doing something strictly on my own."

Aside from privacy there are other reasons why people hide their therapy ventures.

Conscientious Loved Ones Who Invite, Then Blockade, The Truth

Some adults refrain from telling their parents they are in therapy, because they fear they'll be viewed as "sick," "selfish," "trendy," or "troubled." Coming from families where differences were dangerous, they maintain self-esteem by shielding themselves from anticipated criticism. Having been critiqued too many times, these clients are conditioned to expect harsh judgment from their parents.

Nevertheless, many young adults, excited by personal

explorations, tell their relatives that they are "seeing someone" about their problems. They later regret having been so open. Although they know that their parents or partners are *trying* to be supportive, they hear innuendos which convey suspicion, anger, and disrespect. The following outcries have come from clients caught in such situations:

"I wish my parents could trust me. If they did, I would share more of my feelings with them. Sometimes their distrust makes me feel untrustworthy."

"I wish my husband could *respect* me for who I really am. I have great difficulty respecting myself. When he can't respect my therapy, I feel distant from him."

"I wish my parents could honor my decisions—even if my choices are different from theirs. If they respected my therapy, I'd be able to answer their questions more honestly. As it is, I give short answers and change the topic."

"I wish my spouse could just let me be sad—distant, silent, angry—without taking my moods so personally. Unless I can really act happy, I just don't speak."

"I wish they could listen without interrupting, getting mad, feeling hurt, or implying I'm ungrateful. They ask me to tell them about my life and therapy. When I try, their emotions erupt. That's why I don't talk about 'real' things with my parents."

"I wish my parents were happier—healthier, more resilient. I feel sad when I'm around them. Sometimes I feel guilty for being happy. So I just act somber when I'm with them."

"I wish my parents would stop making negative comments about my being in therapy. Sometimes they even attack *you*. When they do this, I feel angry and distant—like there's this bridge that will never be crossed."

Some parents and partners, confident in themselves and their loved ones, embrace the uniqueness of their children and partners. They respect boundaries and intuitively know when not to intrude. Others *attempt* to display affection and interest, but their anxieties prevent meaningful interchanges. The unique characteristics of each relationship and family will affect the degrees to which adults in therapy request information, expose vulnerabilities, and engage in meaningful dialogues about the therapeutic process.

Thus the parental or partner's question, "How can I help?" is affected by their relationship with their loved one or child, the nature of their loved one's difficulties, and personality. There is no simple answer to the question, "How can I help?" Moving on with one's own life, honoring personal privacy, and displaying quiet, respectful concern are universal features of all supportive relationships.

SPECIAL TIMES AND SITUATIONS

There are several circumstances which may precipitate your engagement in an adult child's or partner's therapeutic struggles. For a parent, these situations are more likely to occur if your son or daughter is unmarried or unpartnered, lives nearby or with you, or displays perplexing emotions and symptoms.

Getting Started—The Pre-Therapy Abyss

We've discussed the types of issues that bring people to the therapist's office. As mentioned earlier, most individuals don't initiate treatment unless they are psychologically sophisti-cated or have pursued other avenues to alleviate their suffering. Because the concept of therapy may be terrifying, some people need a friend or relative to help them take the first step. When initiating treatment, many adults worry that they will discover they are "crazy" or fundamentally "defective."

"Not me! Not me!" wept one woman whose friend had suggested counsel. I'd have a nervous breakdown if I saw a shrink! All that introspection! I'd go crazy!"

Many types of resistance prevent troubled adults from seeking professional help and prolong unnecessary suffering. I call this period the "pre-therapy abyss."

Even though a parent is aware that an adult child is upset and that professional assistance might be indicated, she or he may hesitate to intervene. After all, the child is an adult, and the parent does not want to intrude on personal decisions. At times like this, parents who respect the therapeutic process may wonder:

> *Should I say something? If so, what?*
> *Should I get the names of some therapists?*
> *How would she react if I intervened?*
> *Is this my business or not?*
> *Would she get mad or feel that I'm treating her like a*
> *baby if I implied she's stuck on a problem?*

The fact that a parent is asking these questions implies something is awry. Yet, the parent doesn't know what to do. The parent can't pretend everything's normal when twenty-five year-old Jesse stays in his room all day half drunk. The parent, having spent his or her life safeguarding the well-being of the family, can't sit by without "doing something."

One obvious first step is to discuss your questions with a professional. "Am I overreacting?" "Am I seeing a problem that doesn't exist?" "Is Dorothy just temporarily depressed, or is she at risk?" "Am I doing something to provoke these angry outbursts?" An expert can help you to sort out how serious the problem is, whether you are part of the problem, and what, if anything, might be done to intervene.

One thing not to do is nothing.

I am reminded of Jennifer, a depressed woman who initiated treatment in her early thirties.

One day, as Jennifer was regaining her strength, she burst into tears. "If only my mother had let me see a therapist when I was twenty!" she wept. "I know I shouldn't blame Mom, but I'd asked her about getting help and she just said there was nothing wrong with me."

Jennifer continued to weep in rage. "So I wasted eight years being miserable. I accomplished nothing! If only Mom had helped. Boy, if I ever have kids, I'll help them find a therapist before I help them find a college. The earlier you start, the easier it is. Eight wasted years!" Jennifer pounded her fists on the arms of the big leather chair.

Unfortunately, not all young adults are responsive to the idea of therapy—especially if the suggestion comes from a parent. However, the advantage of having a family member recommend treatment is that the problem remains relatively private. I recently received a call from Alex, a man who wondered whether I might meet with his twenty-three-year-old son, Fletcher. He recounted this story:

"My son and I were at the game last Saturday when my ex-wife, Fletcher's mother, walked up to the refreshment stand with yet *another* lover. My 'ex' has dated many men since our divorce, and it's rumored that she's promiscuous, but I don't know. So there was my son, standing next to his mother and her date at the hot dog stand.

"Fletch whispered, 'Pop, I've gotta go home!'

"'But son,' I said, 'it's only half time.'

"'I've gotta leave,' pleaded Fletch, pulling me towards the exit. I could see he was holding back tears. We got to the car and Fletch broke down. He said, 'Pop, I'm a wreck, a miserable wreck. I don't trust women and I know it's because of Mom. I'm shaky and weird all the time.'

"So I said, 'Fletch, how about seeing a therapist?'

"'You've got to be crazy, Pop!' he almost screamed.

"But this morning he called me. He said he'd talked with his roommate who's in therapy, and asked if I knew the names of some therapists. That's when I called you."

This story describes the automatic resistance a son or daughter may feel to a parent's suggestion that therapy might help. It was Fletch's friend, finally, who convinced him to pursue the idea. A parent may not receive the credit, but as parents they can "plant the seeds" and hope something happens.

If you as a parent are concerned with the safety or happiness of a son or daughter, you may suggest the idea of therapy. "It's worked for others," you might remark. "So there's no reason why therapy can't work for you." If you maintain a relaxed, easy-going manner, you are less likely to alarm or alienate your child. In addition, you can ask a trusted friend to obtain the names of qualified clinicians. Although an adult child, like Fletch, may proclaim that you are "crazy," your efforts won't be wasted. Many people enter the therapist's office because of a concerned relative or friend who cared enough to do the initial spadework. A phone number may be all that is needed at a desperate moment.

An adult child may not like the fact that the "therapy idea" came from you. He or she may feel insulted, offended, or outraged. And, if therapy is pursued, you may not receive the credit.

For four years a mother had "gently" suggested the idea of therapy to her agitated daughter. Sherry had rebuffed her mother, calling her "nuts," "out of it," and "ridiculous."

One spring day, Sherry's older brother strolled into her slovenly apartment. "Hey, Sher," he snorted, "what ya doing in this hovel? You're wasting your brain and your life, kid, living like this. You're too smart, little girl. Here's a name. Give this little shrink a little call. She's cool. Now *do it* and I'll be back to check you out!" Big brother gave his kid sister a phone number on a slip of paper, an affectionate punch on the shoulder, and left the apartment.

Sherry called the "little shrink" the next day. She never found out that her mother had given her brother the slip of paper.

Therapeutic Crises

"You'll *never* find me calling my parents," said my 'independent' client Mike. "Never! Never again!" He laughed. "That would spell defeat. Like D-E-F-E-A-T! I'm not using drugs or drinking. No! I've got my wife Cherie. My last call home has been made!"

Several months later I received a call at eleven at night from Mike.

"I'm calling from my folks' house," he apologized. "I was doing just fine until Cherie didn't come home. So my mind started racing. 'Oh my God, she's dead . . . a car accident!' My head started swirling, I couldn't catch my breath. It was the worst panic attack I've ever had. I kept thinking, 'Cherie is dead.' I started getting faint and all I could think of was to call my folks—Dad was over in five minutes.

"They told me to call you. I guess it's my old death fear again. Mom and Dad were great. You know, it's just like always: No questions asked."

Mike is right. His parents are "great." They genuinely respect Mike for the heroic changes he's already made in his life. They keep themselves available for him. They don't ask belittling questions, nor do they sabotage the "therapeutic alliance."

The "therapeutic alliance" is the active, positive *working* relationship that is established between therapist and client over time. Grounded in trust and understanding, the therapeutic alliance holds client and clinician together during the most challenging phases and "crises" of therapy. In suggesting that Mike call his therapist, his parents were supporting the therapeutic alliance.

There are any number of therapeutic crises that may occur during a client's treatment. Therapeutic crises, as opposed to other life crises (such as a back injury or financial disaster), involve issues peculiar to the therapeutic process. Typically, they are growth enhancing. Most crises are minor—like the day the saxophonist forgot his dream and was afraid of his therapist's presumed anger. Other crises are major—such as times when the client is so outraged at the therapist that he or she threatens to quit therapy. These are treatment related phenomena which rarely involve the parent.

For example, Mike's anxiety attack was a reenactment of the feelings he'd had many years ago when his mother had collapsed on the living room floor. Mike, then age four, had decided that his mother was dead. He'd also concluded that he, therefore, would also die. As he reworked his infantile terrors in therapy, he became more relaxed. With time and medication, his anxiety attacks faded away and he no longer equated his wife's late arrivals home from work with "death."

Some clients occasionally display overt symptoms which will engage a parent or friend. Such events may include suicidal threats, prolonged withdrawals to the bedroom, panic and anxiety attacks, angry outbursts, or crying spells. With an adult son or daughter who lives nearby and who may occasionally be seized by symptoms, the parent may wonder whether and how to intervene.

Assume that regardless of the severity of the emotional outburst, the therapist will understand the precipitating event and the underlying issues involved. This is one reason why frequent sessions are of value. The better the therapist is able to "track" the client's moods, fantasies, actions and thoughts, the better position she or he will be in to make sense of clinical surprises.

Partners and parents of adults who suffer severe mental illness such as schizophrenia or bi-polar disorders are often called in to assist during crises. These people, whose issues will be discussed later, are unsung heroes who appear at all hours in emergency rooms, admit adult children to hospitals, and carefully monitor medications.

If you are the parent of less fragile offspring, you may never witness such extreme crises. Your adult child is coping with manageable problems. But "manageable" does not mean "easy." Even functional adults like Mike swerve through periods of extreme emotional fragility.

Another form of "therapeutic crisis"—a crisis related to the treatment process—occurs when the client is angry at the clinician and wants to quit therapy. Unless a parent or partner has clear evidence that the therapist is dysfunctional or behaving in an unprofessional way, the person's involvement will be minimal.

"I'm quitting therapy," Jonah shouted at his partner.

"What's that?" asked Jackie as she glanced up from the newspaper.

"It's obvious that my therapist doesn't care about me. She's taking another vacation! Ten days this time! And right before my exams! If she really cared, she'd stick around. So if she doesn't care about me, then I don't care about her."

Jonah was so angry he ripped his physics assignment into shreds.

"When was her last vacation, Jonah?" asked his partner after putting her paper aside.

"Just eight months ago, and now she's taking off again. I can't wait to see the look on her face tomorrow when I tell her I'm quitting!"

"Everyone needs a vacation," his partner said. "I know it's hard on you when your therapist leaves town."

Jonah calmed down, tossed his book on the floor, and departed through the front door to take a walk.

His partner was doing her best. She stayed calm. She didn't attack the therapist. She didn't criticize Jonah for feeling angry. She offered a reality-based idea: everyone needs a vacation. Jonah's anger at the therapist's non-availability echoed how hurt and angry he was years ago about his mother's emotional absenteeism. The degree of Jonah's anger indicates he is working on an important issue and is deeply invested in the therapeutic relationship. His anger is a cover for his attachment to his therapist and his hurt feelings: after all, no one really cares. Although his conclusions are inaccurate, this is Jonah's current emotional reality. If an adult child or partner draws a parent or companion into this type of crisis, the person can help by staying calm, acknowledging the reality of his or her angry feelings, and encouraging the other person to explore the meanings of his conclusions with the therapist. At such a potentially productive moment, quitting therapy would be most unfortunate. In fact, such a precipitous departure would reenact, in reverse form, what had happened to Jonah as a child. "You mentally abandoned me—so I'll abandon you!" He would be "acting out" his feelings instead of talking them through in order to gain insight and mastery over his separation anxieties.

If your adult child suffers an exacerbation of symptoms during therapy, remember Mike and Jonah. Their loved ones were available, respectful, non-intrusive, and responsive. They provided a safe and quiet environment for retreat. By encouraging anxious Mike to call his therapist, Mike's father conveyed respect for the privacy of his son's therapy. By commenting to angry Jonah that "it's hard when your therapist leaves town," Jonah's partner displayed empathy. Both people conveyed trust in their loved ones and respect for the competence of their clinicians.

The Crisis of Competitive Needs

Parents and partners are people, too! Partners are there through thick and thin. Parents raise their children from infancy until adulthood—at times against great odds. They would like to feel appreciated for their heroic efforts. Tired from child rearing, parents often yearn for quiet and rest.

"It's my turn now," wept Alicia Owens, fifty-nine. Two of her grown children have moved back to the area. One is using drugs and the other is depressed and unemployed. "I've raised my kids, I've done my work. I want peace and quiet. No more problems, please!"

Mrs. Owens' request is understandable. She wants time for her painting and writing. She yearns to travel. However, she can't extract herself from the ongoing needs of her adult children! Her own needs for quietude compete with her impulse to rescue her children. Unless Mrs. Owens finds a way to reestablish her priorities, she will find herself enmeshed in a series of serious crises.

Some critics of recent child-rearing techniques stress that parents have rendered too much power to their young children. Impelled to please and do things "right," parents attempt to respond to every request. Fearful of damaging their children, many parents don't offer firm discipline. They neither set limits on what they can offer nor set roadblocks against inappropriate behavior. Have they failed to convey that for the home (and the world) to run smoothly, everyone must pitch in?

The adult children of these indulgent parents often appear entitled and ungrateful, but their unhappiness is as deep as their shocked awakening to the demands of adult life.

In responding to every child's need, the child-bound parent loses his or her sense of identity and personal authority. Children need and *like* to know that their efforts at home are valuable. Feeling needed provides the child a sense of place and importance. A child's belief in his or her essential worth will later be applied within the broader social world.

I mention this pattern of child rearing because so much of this book highlights the wishes of the offspring over the wishes of the parent or partner. Now it's time for you to review your privileges and rights!

Crises arise when people compete for each other's attention. In many over-stressed families, conflicts arise from competitive neediness. The symptoms and self-absorption that may accompany a person's psychotherapy journey should not preclude his or her sensitivity to a partner or parent's feelings and life phase. The loved one in therapy is likely to overlook the wishes of the parent or partner if the other person doesn't know and express his or her desires clearly.

Hopefully, the therapeutic journey of a partner or child will affect the family or relationship in positive ways. However, preoccupation with the therapy may seduce parents or partners into overlooking their own needs for sustenance.

Regardless of whether your adult child or partner is or is not in therapy, you as a person have your own plans, ambitions, and projects. Sometimes you may be too tired to stay up late talking about conflicts and memories with your loved one. Sometimes you may be asked questions you don't have time to answer. Sometimes, despite your best efforts, you may be too preoccupied to offer immediate emotional support.

A parent or partner has the right to state limits. Establishing boundaries to your generosity may be just what the other person unknowingly seeks: a role model for setting limits. If adult children or partners refuse to accept the reasonable limits of others, they can appear ungrateful and selfish. Have your loved ones equated your efforts at limit-setting with total rejection or selfishness?

Bernice

"What you're saying intrigues me," I said to a troubled young veterinarian. "But I'm afraid our time is up for today."

"Our time is up?" Bernice protested. "I've hardly started talking! Furthermore, I was late."

"Our time is over for today," I repeated quietly. "Can we return to this topic on Friday?"

"Friday!" Bernice exclaimed. "That's three days away!" She remained planted in her chair. "You don't have anything else to do. I want to continue."

"Our time is up for today."

"Listen," Bernice responded angrily, "it's not my fault I was late; plus, I know this is just your lunch hour. I want to finish what I was saying."

"I'm afraid our time is up," I said gently, while reflecting on my need to return several emergency calls.

Bernice rose grudgingly. Leaving, she muttered, "I knew you weren't really interested."

Bernice is not a "spoiled" lady; nor was she a "spoiled" child. After her mother died, she was raised by an elderly aunt who hired a succession of nannies to care for her. Aunt Emelda was a busy union leader and often harsh. Yet she had a lively spirit and Bernice relied on her for affection. Aunt Emelda's comings and goings from the house were abrupt. If Bernice called from a friend's house, Emelda would sound impatient and hang up without a goodbye. If Bernice was leaving for school, Aunt Emelda would nearly "push" her out the door.

When they would sit down for tea, Bernice never knew when Aunt Emelda would suddenly grow tense and, without explanation, leave the room. Since Aunt Emelda did not have the ability to set firm but loving limits, Bernice, as an adult, both dreads and resents all forms of limit-setting. Equating others' departures, limits, and boundaries with memories of profound deprivation from Aunt Emelda, Bernice reacts with indignation.

On the other hand, setting limits in a loving way need not take much time, as is the case with Diane and her mother.

Diane and Her Mom

"Mom, can you explain why you used to buy Debbie new clothes but you only give me hand-me-downs?"

Diane's mother is rushing to a doctor's appointment.

"Mom, did you hear me?" Twenty-five-year-old Diane is taking the day off from work. She has decided to relax at Mom's house.

Diane's mom stops searching for her keys. She needs to be on time, but Diane's question is painful.

"That's an important question, Diane," her mom replies, looking into Diane's pale, angry eyes. "I'd like to give it some thought and talk tonight, but right now I'm almost late for Dr. Bradley. Can we talk about it later?"

"Okay, Mom."

Diane shuts the door as her mother rushes down the steps. That night, after dinner, Diane's mother makes sure to re-introduce the topic.

By setting her limits lovingly, Diane's mother stated a fact: she really needed to go. She also conveyed concern for her daughter's feelings and the importance of her question. She remembered to continue the discussion later. "Let's talk later" has no value if "later" never comes.

A number of situations may arise during a person's therapy which could precipitate a crisis of competitive needs. The following situations are examples of when a caring parent should set clear limits.

Adult children or partners may ask questions which the other people in his or her life are not ready to answer. A response at that moment might be painful or injurious, or might intrude on privacy. The need to postpone answering may be greater than the person in therapy's immediate need to know.

A partner or adult child may become verbally abusive of a parent or loved one through name-calling and character bashing. In this case, a parent or partner should leave the room thus forcing the other person to abandon the attack for now. A partner or parent's need to protect his or her dignity is greater than a child's need to confront the parent or a person's need to confront his significant other in a destructive manner.

A parent or partner may be blamed for events that never occurred. A parent or partner's need to state his or her view of the truth is as great as the other person's need to convince the parent or partner that he or she is correct.

In one instance, an adult son, living at home, assumes that the parent should do all the housework. He justifies this expectation by claiming that his non-medical "symptoms" (for example, fatigue, anxiety, listlessness) or his mission to "make up for lost time" prevent him from helping out. The parent's need for practical assistance in the home is greater than the adult child's need to be babied.

Let us suppose that a wife comes home drunk or drugged and expects the partner to call her boss to cover for her absence. The partner's need to refuse this request is greater than the loved one's need for an alibi.

These types of situations are typical in families or relationships where people lack courtesy and respect. These are not situations that arise only when people are in therapy. In fact, problems of these types are *less* likely to arise in families or relationships where adult children or partners are reflecting on their behaviors in disciplined ways. These people are more likely to appear to be merely self-centered and preoccupied.

I hope that by reading this book, you as a parent or partner are trying to honor yourself and your loved one in therapy more fully. Can you lovingly state your own rights and limits— just as the person in therapy is learning to do?

The "Impaired Therapist" Crisis

Dear Mom and Dad,

I know you don't know much about therapy, but I need your advice. The psychologist I've been seeing was recommended by my grad school's counseling service, and he's really nice. As much as I like him, though, I'm beginning to wonder if he's behaving professionally. He's been doing some weird things. Like, he's told me not to tell anybody that he wants to hire me as his secretary. He knows I need a job and may just be trying to help, but I can't understand why I'm not supposed to talk about it. Then he asked me to run out and buy lunch for him after my last therapy hour. He said I could buy a lunch for myself, too, and eat with him before I left for class. A few other things have happened which I don't want to write down. Since he's kind to me, I can only assume he knows what he's doing. But I feel uneasy. I don't want to stop therapy, but I'm beginning to dread going. I'm getting more—not less—anxious. Do you think my therapist has my best interests in mind?

Love,
Kristy

P.S. Please don't tell anybody what I've told you.
P.P.S. Please call me Friday night.

Kristy's parents are dog trainers who don't know much about the ethics of the mental health profession. They made an appointment with their town's clinical social worker, who reviewed with them the following principles of professional behavior:

1. It is inappropriate for a psychotherapist to be person ally involved with a patient outside of the treatment hour. This prohibition includes both social and most extracurricular professional activities.
2. It is inappropriate for a clinician to be sexually involved with a patient. This includes erotic hugging and touching, as well as intercourse.
3. It is inappropriate for a professional to exploit the vulnerability of a patient in order to gratify the clinician's personal wishes.

Kristy had waited five months before writing to her parents. By then she had become so confused and anxious that her campus doctor had prescribed high doses of tranquilizers without knowing the causes for her agitation. Her symptoms were a result of her dysfunctional relationship with Dr. Z. We call these symptoms "iatrogenic." Iatrogenic symptoms are induced by a clinician's inappropriate words or behaviors.

When Kristy's parents called their daughter on Friday night they expressed concern and stated that she would have to stop seeing her therapist because he was clearly violating the principles of the mental health profession. Hearing this, Kristy burst into tears.

"But I don't want to stop seeing him," she protested. "He's kind, he's loving, and he knows me so well by now! I'll just tell him to behave more properly."

"No, Kristy, that's not good enough," her father responded quietly. "Stop seeing him. We'll help you to find another therapist."

After Kristy initiated treatment with a second therapist,

she spent an entire year recovering from the distrust, anger, and confusion created by her first therapist's behavior. The most painful aspect of the transition was her grief over losing such a "nice man." She had invested two years of work with him. She had thought he had taken a special interest in her without realizing that his interest was based primarily on his own needs—not hers.

Kristy was fortunate that she could confide in her parents. She was smart enough to know that something was wrong. Through her parents' intervention she was able to move on to constructive therapy.

Although crises like these are relatively rare, they may be the source of lasting pain and conflict for the innocent client. Assessing whether or not a psychotherapist has or has not been unprofessional may be difficult for several reasons.

First, the client may be misinterpreting a highly ethical clinician's warmth as "seductive." If this is the case, the client is dealing with a therapeutic distortion (or transference) issue. This misperception, obviously, is not related to the therapist's misconduct.

Second, the patient may become emotionally attached to an unethical therapist and therefore deny the therapist's impairment. If the therapist is verbally or physically seductive, the client may feel temporarily flattered or special. Or, too naive to detect disrespect, the client may be unaware of improprieties. Sensitive to loss, another client may decide to continue treatment—despite its problems—in order to avoid an excruciating separation. For these reasons, clients often deny improprieties and wait too long to terminate the association. When they do ask for help from parents or friends, they may refuse the very advice they sought. "But, Daddy," wept Kristy, "I don't want to stop seeing him!"

Third, some highly ethical therapists will offer a comforting goodbye hug to a grieving client or gently touch the shoulder of a withdrawn client to convey their presence. If there is any physical contact, it should be solely for therapeutic and humane reasons. Erotic behavior in any form generated by the therapist's wish for gratification is strictly inappropriate, unethical, and, in some states, illegal. Since boundary issues are complex, many therapists limit physical contact to a warm handshake.

If you are concerned about the ethics of your loved one's psychotherapist, you must intervene! Like Kristy's parents, you will want to respect the cues, conflicts, and complexity of this delicate matter. If, after professional consultation, it becomes clear that your child is working with someone who is either mentally disturbed or unprofessional, you must protect your child! Start by helping the person in therapy to find a better therapist. Try to proceed gently, respectfully, and promptly.

You and your loved one may also decide to protect others by filing a formal complaint to the clinician's professional licensing board.

Fortunately, therapist's improprieties occur only rarely. All professional groups contain their share of impaired workers, and the mental health profession is no exception.

Financing Therapy

Because of the high cost of quality therapy, an adult child may ask for a parent's financial support. Families respond in different ways to these requests. Some parents are in no position to pay, others say they will help with part of the cost, and a few parents pay the full therapy fee. Regardless of the parents' ability and willingness to offer financial support, a number of issues often surround the family's financial involvement in the therapeutic process.

DID I DO SOMETHING WRONG?

Matty

The daughter of a California millionaire, Matty arrived late for her first consultation. She described an unhappy vagabond life in which she had drifted from town to town and job to job. She said that nothing she had done had seemed very important. She felt lost and wondered about going to art school. When asked how she would finance her treatment, she said, "Just send the bills to Daddy."

I inquired why the bill should be mailed to her father.

"Oh," she responded, "he pays for my car, my rent, my dates and entertainment. So—you can just send the bill to Daddy."

When I asked her why I might not send the bills to her, Matty looked up with winsome blue eyes and responded, "I'm not responsible. I'd probably forget to send him the bills. Here's Daddy's address. Just mail the bills to him."

I responded that I would send the bills to her and that she would understand, with time, why this might be in her best interest.

Without knowing it, Matty had defined her first therapeutic issues: overdependence on her father, submissiveness, and personal irresponsibility. If a parent is able to finance part or all of an adult child's treatment, the bills may be sent to and paid by the son or daughter. Whether the parent establishes a separate "therapy" account or sends money to an adult child on a regular basis, the business negotiations of the treatment ideally occur between the therapist and the client.

After being in therapy for a year, Matty, whose parents are wealthy, had obtained a job in a beauty shop and, for the third time, was applying to art school. Having taken lessons in oil painting, she had developed an impressive portfolio. Hopeful and directed, she was an enthusiastic client.

In the midst of this progress, she arrived for therapy in

tears one day. "Daddy says he won't pay for my therapy any more," she wept. "He says he's decided I should see a different kind of professional, maybe a vocational counselor."

When I asked what had precipitated this turn of events, Matty replied, "For the first time in my life I got irritated at Daddy. He'd called me a 'good for nothing,' because I want to be an artist. So I told him that he shouldn't talk to me that way. Then he said my therapist was turning me into an artist and he wanted to pay for a different kind of therapist."

Matty's dilemmas demonstrate the types of problems that can arise if a client's parents finance therapy. If parents are helping to pay the bill, they may assume they can oversee the work and approve the final "product." Whereas this monitoring might be effective during a college education, it will interfere with—if not obliterate—the success of therapy.

Once a loved one has selected a qualified therapist, it's the person's job to regulate the ways he or she wants to change and grow. He or she must define central issues, comply with the therapist's policies, and attend sessions—without having to "report back to Daddy," or to a partner. Generous parents want to help their children. However, if a parent has an unconscious need to control or manipulate the adult child, this tendency often becomes evident in relation to financial matters. Matty's father appeared to feel threatened that his daughter was becoming a competent, assertive woman. No longer his obliging little girl, she finally refused to let him control her thoughts, loyalties, and professional direction.

Four months after terminating her therapy because of lack of money and a large overdue balance, Matty returned to my office. Her father had held true to his word and rescinded all payment offers. In the meantime, Matty had been accepted to art school with a fellowship and had acquired a technical job which would help her to finance therapy.

"It would have been nice if Dad had been more understanding," she said with a smile, "but it feels terrific to pay my own bills." Matty handed me her personal check. Her name was signed with artistic elegance.

Most parents who assist with therapy costs are respectful of their offspring's boundaries. They want to help—with no strings attached or questions asked. Without their help, their sons and daughters would not be able to afford high-quality therapy. Most parents are resilient enough to survive the unexpected changes in their adult children, including ever-expanding degrees of independence. Many relatives help out financially—without demanding a specific "outcome."

HOW CAN A PARENT OR PARTNER HELP?

In this chapter, I have tried to respond to the questions of parents and partners who want to "help" but don't know how. As you have seen, some situations clearly warrant involvement. For example, you may want to locate the names of good therapists to help your adult child or partner "get started." Or you might be called to the emotional rescue. If your adult child lives at home, you may be challenged by new and unwelcome questions and behaviors. Most of the time, however, your loved ones will move through therapy quietly. You will not be called upon to assist, because the person in therapy is becoming expert at helping him or herself. Psychotherapy is effective because of the privacy it affords.

In the meantime, your lives—separate and shared—proceed as usual. Birthdays and holidays are celebrated. New jobs are accepted. People come together, separate, and come together again.

How can you help? You can fully immerse yourself in the tides of personal and family life. By plunging into your own passions when you are alone, you will be a more enthusiastic participant when the troops rally again.

"How rapidly time goes by," commented Rosanne's mother as she rose from the couch and hobbled toward the "care" package. She scooted her walker toward Rosanne's basket of sweets. "When you were little, I didn't know whether I was coming or going. Now that you're grown, I look back and think 'where did the time go?' I like having time now, to make pretty things for you. Have another sugar cookie."

Mrs. Rosenberg's arthritic fingers drew a second fig from Rosanne's package. "You know, next week, I'll make a basket for myself!" chuckled Mrs. Rosenberg as she served herself a macaroon.

It's never too late to sweeten up your life.

CHAPTER 8

HEROIC HELPERS, COURAGEOUS CLIENTS: SPECIAL CHALLENGES . . . SPECIAL COURAGE

Since 'tis nature's law
to change,
Constancy alone
is strange.

John Wilmot, Earl of Rochester

All people suffer tragedy and pain, and most of us find coping strategies that ensure long-term stability. Psychotherapy is one of many methods for assisting the basically hearty to become healthier. With effort, therapy, and the loving support of family and friends, these people sail on to "the new."

Theirs are the tales of the fortunate.

JUST IN CASE . . . OF SEVERE MENTAL DISABILITY

Some are not so fortunate. Thousands of people cope with severe mental disability. Less resilient than their peers for whom emotional relief is more easily accessible, these mentally disabled people require special courage and special help.

When severe mental illness strikes a loved one, it hits us hard. Relatives and friends become confused by the changes they witness in the person. The early signs of mental illness often emerge during young adulthood and are sometimes hard to decipher.

The good news is that new treatments and early interventions have been found for those struggling with severe disorders.

If you are the parent or loved one of someone you think may be suffering from mental deterioration, you will want to keep a number of concepts in mind.

The Early Signs of Serious Emotional Disturbance

First, it's important to know that everyone experiences a little depression or anxiety—at times. Simply because a loved one seems more reserved, introspective, or depressed than usual, you need not assume that he or she is seriously disturbed. Many life changes require new adaptation, withdrawal, or heightened emotional response.

Second, there are questions to ask when we are concerned about someone. These include:

Has there been a strange deterioration in general functioning or thinking for no apparent reason? For example, Heather had always been a straight A student until her last year of college when she stopped attending classes, failed half her courses, and spent much of her time closeted in her dormitory room. She could give no reasons for these changes except that she "wasn't happy." Her "strange" talk included bizarre references to "UFO's."

Has job performance deteriorated? Some people change jobs frequently with the explanation that the work was "too hard" or that there was too much stress. While erratic work behavior is typical for some otherwise healthy people, it can be a danger sign. A radical shift in job performance for inexplicable reasons, especially when accompanied by other indications of instability may indicate mental decompensation.

Have social activities changed? If previously cherished relationships have turned chaotic, you may question the cause of these upheavals. A gregarious person who always enjoyed parties and social gatherings who now isolates himself may be sending warning signals.

Has there been a change in your loved one's temperament? An eager and outgoing personality who suddenly becomes reclusive and exquisitely sensitive to criticism may be showing signs of mental difficulty. The opposite pattern would be that of a usually sensitive and brooding person who all of a sudden seems "too happy," "too euphoric," or "too giddy."

Has your friend or relative lost his or her resilience? Everyone has bad days—even bad years. Yet, as stated by Dr. Brian Schulman, a Maryland psychiatrist, most key in the assessment of severe mental disturbances is the "loss of resilience." A person who weeps without provocation, "falls apart," retreats to the bedroom, cannot eat, and does not heal, may have lost his or her resilience.

People who find themselves deteriorating attempt to "get hold of themselves." Their inner worlds feel different, strange, confusing. They are unable to label their feelings and are often secretive about bizarre thoughts. Incapable of explaining to themselves what has gone wrong, they may isolate themselves in places that are quiet and unstimulating. It's terrifying to feel that you are not your old self and to experience life with such raw and fluid fragility. Individuals who undergo these types of changes are legitimately self-protective.

The parents, partners, and friends of these suffering people may, however, deny that their loved one is "breaking down."

What Can a Parent or Loved One Do in the Event of Potentially Severe Disturbances?

If, indeed, your loved one *is* mentally deteriorating, remember that he or she is frightened and confused. Before you place your first call to a mental health professional, be a sharp observer of the changes taking place. The more specifically you can describe the symptoms, the more useful your consultant can be. Have you noticed changes in diet, sleep, or the content of your partner or child's speech? Have you noticed behaviors that are atypically aggressive, bizarre, or volatile? Isolative or withdrawn? Before you meet or talk with a mental health expert, observe and take note of your adult child's or partner's moods and actions.

As you inquire among friends for the names of qualified clinicians, you will want reassurance that the consultant will be respectful of both your partner's and your family's distress. Whenever a loved one is physically injured or ill, all family members are affected. Mental illness is no different.

If your consultant agrees that your concerns warrant attention, you will be encouraged to help your adult child contact a specialist. But your son or daughter, already fearful, may resist the first appointment.

Your consistency, gentleness, patience, and optimism will help your loved one agree to a family session. Try not to target the child as the source of the problem. Explain to him or her that you have a "number of family concerns" to discuss with an expert. You have made an appointment and you would appreciate everyone's participation.

Once you, as a family, are in the consulting room, your clinician will be in a position to assess the nature of your adult child's—and your family's—situation. In addition to recommending appropriate interventions for your son or daughter, the consultant may recommend several family sessions. You will need advice if your child displays signs of serious mental disability. As stated in *Harvard's Mental Health Newsletter*, "recent studies have shown that family therapy or family management improves the symptoms and reduces the burden substantially."

Indeed, if your son or daughter is mentally disturbed, his or her condition is a family concern. Phyllis Vine's book, *Families in Pain*, describes the courage and conflicts of parents, siblings, and other family members as they struggle to support their emotionally fragile relatives. Few adults live untouched by the special challenges of those who cope with chronic mental disorders. Schizophrenia alone is estimated to affect from 0.5 to 3 percent of the population. Many other conditions, although less severe, also require the committed investment of families. Groups like the National Alliance for the Mentally Ill (NAMI) offer education and other services to family members of mentally disturbed individuals.

Although a partner or child, if showing marked changes in behavior and mood, may be experiencing a transitional crisis, parents and spouses should educate themselves about the more serious conditions which require immediate intervention. If your loved one is struggling with mental illness, he or she needs your help. Serious conditions *do* become "family matters." Until our communities can finance better services for the emotionally fragile, mental illness will pose special challenges for immediate family members.

If your relative or loved one is disintegrating rapidly or becoming psychotic, take him or her to a hospital for emergency consultation. The more you deal with your loved one's distress in a calming, non-judgmental manner, the less he or she will feel frightened by your recommendations. No one should *ever* feel ashamed of psychiatric symptoms or illness. Stand tall as you walk with your loved one. Be kind. If you can't convey informed optimism to him or her, who will?

Our society is becoming more educated about mental illness and the stamina required by the disabled and their family members. The stories of heroic people who care for the mentally fragile are finally being told.

JUST IN CASE . . . OF SUICIDAL IDEAS

Most of us, during difficult phases in our lives, have exclaimed, "I've had it!" "Why keep trying?" "I give up!"

Most of the time, we really don't mean it. We don't give up. We review our options. Pressures become less intense. We move on with life. We are resilient.

For some people, however, when psychic pain continues too long without relief, a static darkness blots out normal responses to life's options. Despite efforts to crack through a frozen state of immobility, some individuals really mean it when they say, "I've had it." How can we, as parents and friends, discriminate between the safe "I've had it" and that which is dangerous?

If your loved one has become withdrawn, refuses help, feels he or she has suffered a profound loss (whether fantasized or real), and begins to comment that he or she wants to die, you must be attentive and seek assistance. But what if your adult child or partner denies suicidal intentions, and refers only to unhappiness or hopelessness. You feel the paralyzed intensity of the depression in your loved one and grow fearful, but he or she refuses to talk to you.

If your son, daughter, or partner is in psychotherapy and you're concerned about any life or death matter, you will, of course, take emergency measures. Notify the psychotherapist immediately. If the person refuses to contact the clinician him or herself, ask the professional to call your loved one. Stay with that person until he or she has received the call. If you are seriously concerned about some imminent danger, convince your loved one to accompany you to a medical facility.

How can you assess whether your loved one is temporarily depressed as opposed to suicidal? This was the question Mr. Harold Shelly asked when he returned home from a business trip. His son, Danny, had been living in his divorced father's house for the previous ten days. At twenty-five Danny had few friends. He'd returned home from graduate school after failing several courses and losing his girlfriend.

Hal Shelly arrived home at nine o'clock. The house was dark. Entering, he sensed that Danny was present. Yet there were no lights, no music, and no "Welcome home, Pop!"

Hal called to Dan. No response. He searched through the old Victorian mansion and found Danny lying on his bed in a dimly lit room.

"Hey, Danny!" said his father, trying to appear jocular while sensing doom. "Good to see ya!" Hal walked over to Danny's bed.

Dan raised a pale hand and mumbled, "Welcome home, Pop." His face was expressionless.

"What's the matter, Danny?" said his father, trying to humor his son.

"Not much," whispered Danny. "I'm just tired."

"But you're not acting like yourself," said Hal. In earlier times Danny had typically responded to his father coming home with a slap on the back.

"Danny, something is wrong," Hal continued, pulling up a chair.

"Life's not worth living. I'm just depressed," muttered Danny as he rolled towards the wall and away from his dad.

Hal Shelly knew something was wrong. Every time he asked Dan to talk, his son responded that he was just depressed. He said he had been in his room for two days.

If Dan were a young man who used drugs or alcohol, his father would have wondered whether he was drunk or "tripping."

However, Dan neither drank heavily nor used drugs.

"Have you taken something . . . like drugs, pills, or alcohol?" asked Hal, worried that Danny would feel insulted by his question.

"I'm just tired, Pop. Let me be."

If Danny had been in therapy, his father would have called the therapist, but Danny had always believed that only "weak" guys go to therapists. Hall Shelley called his friend Bart, a psychiatrist who lived down the street.

Bart wanted the following information:

Had some event occurred that might have precipitated the emotional withdrawal? Had there been any recent losses—either fantasized or real?

Does Danny use alcohol or drugs. Could he be "tripping?"

Does Danny take medication of any kind? Has he ingested anything that could explain the lethargy?

Has Danny been talking to *anyone*? Close friends or a sibling might know what's bothering Danny and whether he's been talking about his problems—or suicide.

What is the status of Danny's physical health? Could he be physically ill? When was his last checkup?

Has Danny made any references to suicide—to his father or anyone else, at any point in time?

Hal answered "I don't know" or "No" to all of Bart's questions. He repeated that Danny had said, "Life's not worth living." He also told Bart about Danny failing his courses and losing his girlfriend.

Bart suggested that he would call Danny and would come over, unless Danny could suggest someone else with whom he'd rather talk: an old college buddy, a neighborhood friend, or a priest. Danny promised Bart that he would talk to his friend James the next day. He muttered that his father was making too much of a fuss.

That same night, Hal scheduled a consultation with

Bart's colleague, Dr. Hayes. Even if they express irritation when loved ones offer concern, depressed people feel comforted when others initiate action. Hal told his son that he'd made the appointment. He invited Danny to join him the next day. Hal did not leave Danny alone and checked on him frequently during the night. If Danny had displayed signs of having ingested a life-threatening substance, Hal wanted to be ready to call emergency medical help.

Bart stressed to Hal that simply because Danny was withdrawn, there was as yet no specific reason to suspect suicidal intent. People usually allude to suicidal thoughts before attempting the act. "It's rare that people commit suicide without first having communicated those intentions prior to the crisis," states Dr. Barry Bukatman, a Maryland psychiatrist. Bukatman explains that if your child is suicidal, "the relationship that you have with your child is your most useful tool. . . . Use it wisely."

With the encouragement of his father, Bart, and James, Danny hesitantly described the desperation he'd felt all year. During his father's ten-day absence, Danny *had* been thinking about suicide: he'd considered overdosing on non-prescription pills. Luckily, James was in therapy and convinced Dan that it's "okay" to admit you can't solve problems alone. James encouraged Dan to talk about his suicidal ideas and reminded Dan that he could find other ways than suicide to deal with his problems. He helped to reinstate Dan's capacity for hope. At that point, James gave Danny the phone numbers of several qualified therapists.

Now in therapy, Danny can hardly remember the feelings of hopelessness that pervaded his "very bad year." He has started a new school program and enjoys the companionship of a new girlfriend. Staying alone in his father's house had reawakened the terror he'd felt after his parents' divorce. A dignified young man, he feels embarrassed about having caused so much trouble that "very bad" night. He gratefully remembers the week when "Dad saved my life."

Hal had taken the hints of suicide very seriously. So should every parent or partner who discovers a loved one in a similar situation. It is better to err on the side of caution than to risk tragedy.

JUST IN CASE . . . OF DRUG DEPENDENCE OR ADDICTION

"Is my husband using drugs?" asks the wife of a lawyer who was losing his successful practice through his behavior. "If so, what can be done about it?"

"Is our precious daughter becoming an alcoholic?" asks a concerned couple. They have been waiting up till two o'clock in the morning for their daughter, Eliza, who has tried to sneak in through the back door, inebriated.

"How can we know," inquires John Kristie, "whether my brother is just using—or abusing—drugs?"

A November 1989 article titled "Drug Abuse and Dependence—Part II" which appeared in the *Harvard Medical School Mental Health Newsletter* states: "It has become clear that there is no single type of addictive or dependence-prone personality, and no personality traits that reliably indicate in advance who is likely to use or misuse drugs. There seem to be two partially overlapping groups: people who are anxious and depressed . . . and people who are impulsive, rebellious, and antisocial."

Among the warning signs of drug or alcohol abuse is always found a high degree of denial—or the tendency to overlook the addictive behavior. Along with denial are other subtle and dramatic changes in addicts. If loved ones are hiding their addictions, they've probably become isolative or evasive. Fearful of exposure, their drinking and drug use occurs only while they are alone or with others who share the habit. Thus, many drug dependent people avoid non-addicted friends and family members.

Addicted people can become volatile, impulsive, or aggressive. They relinquish activities. Most know that they are ruining their lives. Too much stress, family pressures, too little support, or the need to celebrate are common explanations for their behavior.

Dramatic changes may appear slowly, because the addicted adult tries to hide the habit. On some level—whether conscious or unconscious—the person is terrified. Feeling disorganized, depressed, or desperate, he or she seeks that soothing of another drink or the energy from another sniff. Oscillating between an internal sense of disintegration and the relief afforded by craved-for substances, the afflicted adult runs scared.

If you are concerned that a relative is displaying signs of drug or alcohol addiction, you will feel frustrated by your loved one's denial. As stated in "Drug Abuse and Dependence—Part II": "People who are dependent on drugs often rationalize their use, deny the real cause of their problems, or remember selectively. Besides, alcohol and drug dependence can distort personality, turning Jekylls into Hydes."

As the parents, partners, and peers of people who jeopardize their futures through drug use, you are both powerful and at times powerless. Your power resides in your refusal to support the loved one's destructive behaviors. This means that you will not deny, as he or she is doing, that drugs are being used. Your vigilance, unwillingness to overlook the habit, and non-judgmental confrontations remind your loved one that you are in control.

Your powerlessness is also very real. If recovery is to occur, your loved one must make a serious decision. He or she will have to suffer through the phases of recovery and actively work to maintain sobriety. Your initial powerlessness mirrors the other person's denial and current "powerlessness" over the abused substance.

Parents and partners of addicted people can join support groups such as Alanon. At Alanon meetings, loved ones acquire information, coping strategies, and emotional support. The social stigmas felt by family members are examined and rejected. Passivity is converted into activity. Through participation in meetings, relatives examine their own lives. No longer willing to cooperate with the addicted youth, relatives can become powerful instruments of change.

If you're thinking, "But why should *I* go to meetings? His drinking's not *my* problem," you will have to think again. We are *always* affected by the addictive behaviors of those we love. Often we are part of the problem: not because we're addicted, but because we have become habituated to living in an unhealthy environment. The denial of family members is as understandable as it is dangerous. Relatives don't want to believe that someone who was previously bright and self-confident has resorted to drug use.

Humans safeguard the status quo. Many people are reluctant to "rock the boat." Indeed, in families where one or more members are drug dependent, an active confrontation of these habits *will* and *should* "rock the boat."

"If you love me, you'll pour me a drink," is the message of the alcoholic wife.

"If you love me, Mom," says the addicted son, "you'll *believe* in me—even if you think I use drugs."

"If you love me," implies the alcoholic husband, "you won't notice that I'm coming home drunk and ruining my life."

Obviously, if you really "love" these people, you will love them wisely—not as they request. You will stop colluding with escalating habits. You will stop denying the addictive situation. You will persistently confront loved ones—but only when they are sober. You will take the time to learn coping skills.

By acknowledging problems openly, you demonstrate wise love. Firm wisdom conveys love for your family, for the addicted person, and for yourself. Quite often, you will have to act alone. And you will *feel* alone, until you get outside help.

By contacting a qualified psychotherapist, an addictions counselor, or a self-help group such as Alanon, you will cut through your isolation. To locate a clinician, ask friends or call your local mental health association. For Alanon, AA, and Alateen, consult the phone book.

Just as human beings have a natural tendency to maintain the status quo, we also have a powerful drive to heal. Although many people are unaware of the unconscious mechanisms that promote mental health, the urge for recovery is strikingly apparent among recovering alcoholics and drug users. These individuals must work harder than others to enjoy life. Living "one day at a time," recovering individuals face challenges which their non-addicted peers will never understand. This is one reason why groups like AA are so comforting.

Unfortunately, people who have had less anxious lives can't fully understand the courage of people who must *earn* basic health. The life of a substance survivor requires unusually high degrees of personal honesty and emotional stamina.

Rosie

"Life is much harder for me than for my brothers and sisters," states Rosie, an alcoholic. She has been sober for a year—a scary time for people in recovery. Still insecure, she asks, "Can I keep up my good work? Will I slip?"

"My boyfriend doesn't know," she continues, what it's like for me to go to family parties. I see people having a good time and I feel like a shaky misfit. Just one drink and I could be the life of the party. But I avoid the bar and tremble in the corner. I pray my heart out at times like that.

"My parents don't understand why the only places I feel safe are here and at AA meetings. They couldn't tolerate me when I was drinking. Now they don't like me because I'm fragile.

"People remember me as the messed-up one. They don't see the changes. I still cry a lot. They don't realize that without my crutch, I'm insecure. Maybe my family wants the 'old' me back. At least I could drink my pain away." Pretty Rosie begins to cry. Finally, with a mound of wet hankies on her lap, she says:

"If you get a college education, everyone applauds you. If you're an actress on the stage, everyone cheers you on. If you're successful in business, people say, 'Wow! What a woman!' But if you're a recovering alcoholic, no one cheers except your AA friends. Your relatives just wonder, what the heck does Rosie do with her time? If I tell them I spend time on recovery, they look blank.

"Do you think my parents will ever be proud of me?" Rosie asks.

I do not respond.

"Are *you* proud of me?" she persists.

I smile gently. She knows the answer.

Rosie grins, throws her wet hankies in the trash basket, and takes her leave.

CHAPTER 9

To the Spouse or Partner of a Person in Therapy

What greater thing is there
for two human souls
than to feel that they are joined . . .
to strengthen each other . . .

George Eliot

Gordon and Anthony, both in their thirties, are talking about the football game. They discuss the plays, the penalties, and the disappointing outcome of the season. Then Gordon says, "I dread going home."

"How's that?" asks Anthony.

"Polly had therapy tonight. She always comes home quiet, withdrawn. She never feels like talking . And recently she just cries. I wish she'd get over these crying spells."

"That wasn't how it was when Betsy was in therapy," Anthony says. "She'd come home and couldn't stop talking. All she talked about was her therapist. I'd try to show interest, but I got tired of hearing about the great Dr. D. It was as if I didn't exist."

"Well, I feel *I* don't exist, at times. All the love I offer Polly doesn't sink in. She says she doesn't feel loved. I tell her I love her, but that makes her cry all the more."

"Sounds rough," says Anthony, "but she'll get over it. It's probably just some childhood stuff."

If you are the partner of someone in therapy, you may feel the impact of an intensive treatment process even more than a maturing parent does. Parents' issues are different from those of a partner of a person in therapy. The parent, for example, may feel guilty or self-conscious, fearing indictment. Parents may ask, "Did we do something wrong?" A life review of the parenting years may follow. The partner may share some of these parental concerns—such as fears of criticism or feelings of loss. But since the companion of someone in therapy lives on a daily and intimate basis with the therapy-person, he or she tends to experience a different set of issues.

Partners of people who have been suffering depression, anxiety, and other emotional symptoms are often relieved when therapy is initiated. A heavy, indefinable burden has been relinquished. These partners no longer feel solely responsible for their loved one's recovery. There are fewer fights, fewer tears, and fewer sleepless nights. Knowing that there is someone else out there to help with the distress, partners can defer when problems arise. "Why not talk about that with Dr. D. tomorrow?" suggests Gordon.

Despite the relief they feel, partners can also feel "left out," "displaced," or threatened by the "great Dr. D." The spouse of a person in therapy, after all, isn't just witnessing changes from afar. He or she is living, sleeping, and sharing tasks and social events with the therapied partner all the time. Although many mates are supportive of the therapy process, troublesome issues may arise as time passes. The non-therapy partner may grow to feel that the treatment isn't working, is taking too long, or costs too much. Have your partner's affections been surrendered to the all-admired therapist? No matter how much the "client" tries to protect a spouse, subtle if not dramatic changes will be felt by both companions.

There are common issues that arise in marriages and long-term relationships when therapy becomes part of the partnership. Although I refer most frequently to the marital relationship, this discussion addresses the shared concerns of *any* relationship between two people who live together and are investing their energies in a shared future. The quality and intensity of your concerns will depend on a number of factors. If you are the partner of a person in therapy, your reactions will be affected by personal variables and will change over time.

FACTORS AFFECTING PARTNERSHIP ISSUES

Your Attitudes About the Psychotherapy Process

If you have been in therapy or psychoanalysis yourself, the process of self review isn't foreign. You also know that every therapy has a beginning, a middle, and an end. If your therapy was successful, you can see the broad picture for your partner and know that you can anticipate happier times. You also realize that as "all important" as Dr. D. appears, he or she won't be hovering around your home forever.

On the other hand, if you have never been in treatment or if you view therapy as silly, unnecessary, or self-centered, you may feel alienated if not disapproving. You may not understand how therapy really works. Perhaps your ways of solving life's problems are different from those of your mate. Thus, depending on your attitudes about therapy and your personal style of dealing with difficulties, your reactions to your partner's treatment will be unique to you.

The Type of Treatment Selected by Your Partner

The type of therapy that your partner has chosen will determine the degree to which he or she is preoccupied, emotional, attending to therapy tasks, or ruminating over every word of the "great Dr. D." It will also affect the rapidity with which you see tangible signs of change. Since behavioral and cognitive therapies tend to be short-term and "goal oriented," you may notice behavior or attitudinal changes immediately after your partner's first session. On the other hand, with insight-oriented treatments such as psychodynamic psychotherapy and psychoanalysis, the outward changes will be subtle and gradual.

For example, if the treatment is based exclusively on revising one's "attitudes"—which is the emphasis of cognitive therapy—you may start to hear expressions such as "I can and I will!" instead of the plaintive "I'll *try*" or "I *can't*." Your partner may express new goals. You may be surprised by the apparent rapidity of the preliminary results.

If, on the other hand, behavioral therapy was the treatment of choice, your partner may have devised an elaborate set of rewards for him or herself—such as dinner out or a new fishing rod after smoking that last cigarette. A husband with a flying phobia may be planning weekly trips to the airport with his phobia group. He will spend the first afternoon sitting in a plane reviewing relaxation exercises. On the fifth Saturday, he will take a flight. While obsessing over whether he will panic while airborne, he may sit in the bedroom with earphones, eyes closed and taking deep breaths. You tiptoe quietly around this behavior while thinking to yourself, "If I were he, I'd take the train to Florida!"

By contrast, some therapists give their patients direct instructions to "cry" and "scream" and "role play" scenes. During directive therapies like these, you may peek into your companion's study and see her screaming at an empty chair. Has she gone crazy? you wonder.

A partner in "insight-oriented" psychotherapy (such as psychoanalysis, psychodynamic, or interpersonal therapy) may wear the "face of reflection." In deep thought, your wife may be experiencing her sorrows and distress. While attempting to make sense of her mood swings, she may cry and feel sad, but she will be thinking and making "sense" of her sadness. Eventually, behaviors toward you will become more "considered."

For example, Gordon's wife is at home crying. She's trying to understand why she always cries after therapy especially when Gordon leaves the house. "Am I sad because Gordon went to the game? No, it's because I feel like a lost child. I *hate* leaving my therapist, and I don't have interests of my own. I mustn't pressure Gordon to stay home like an 'all-good' mother so much."

Spouses, lovers, and bosses are often the targets of misdirected anger. One of the greatest causes for relationship difficulties rests upon the fact that we often re-experience in our partners the negative aspects of childhood figures. A loving wife's face may be experienced as unfriendly even though she is truly feeling affectionate. A tired husband's words may be interpreted as "disinterested" even though he's totally engaged in the conversation. These types of misreadings are examples of situations in which feelings towards a childhood figure—or an aspect of a childhood figure—are transferred onto a person in the current relationship. Of *all* the relationships where unwanted transferences occur most intensely, marital or partnered relationships are highest on the list.

Transference refers to the displacement of feelings about someone in the past onto a person in the present. Every new relationship is colored by feelings about other people we know or knew. Within a loving, mutually respectful marital relation-

ship, one of the greatest sources of misunderstanding arises
from the misplacement—or transference—of old feelings about
someone else onto the partner. Equally, an individual may project onto the partner unwanted aspects of his or her own internal
world. Insight-oriented therapies attempt to "rework" old issues
so they will not contaminate current relationships.

Thus, depending on the type of treatment selected, your
partner's level of preoccupation will rise and fall as he or she
moves through the various phases of therapy.

The Severity, Specificity, and Nature Of Your Partner's Problems

The nature and severity of the problems that prompted
your partner to seek treatment will affect your responses to the
therapy. For instance, if your wife, over the years, has become
more and more of a nag and has started therapy to gain mastery
over this trait, you may appreciate her efforts from the start.
Or, if your partner has been withdrawn and lacks his old enthusiasm, you may wonder if you are the cause of the depression.
Many partners of people in therapy willingly support the burden of the process. If you are clear about the purpose of the
treatment and the severity of the suffering, you will appreciate
that these mutually shared sacrifices make sense.

However, if your partner simply states that he or she is
unhappy with life, bored, or "wants more," you may (sometimes correctly) wonder: Is it *me* she's tired of? Will he leave
me? What's the *more* that he wants? If the relationship is
already precarious, the initiation of therapy may be intensely
threatening to the non-therapy partner.

Burdened by the cost of the therapy and the loss of the
partner's total attention, the forgotten spouse may consider
jumping ship. It's difficult to have a loved one confide in someone else. It's difficult not to know what your spouse is thinking

and to be told not to ask. It's frustrating to wait for improvement and to see minimal results. It's lonely to live with a companion who is preoccupied.

Don't forget that it's far more difficult to see a loved one suffer needlessly—without guidance, relief, or hope. Tragedy strikes when treasured relationships become dismantled due to issues unrelated to the here and now. Sometimes therapy is the only choice.

REARRANGED RELATIONSHIPS

The mismatching or realignment of "spatial needs" underlies many couples' conflicts. People often fight about shared versus separate psychic "space." When a partner starts therapy, spatial habits will be temporarily rearranged.

By "personal space," I mean the need for privacy, aloneness, quietude, independence, and self-direction. "Shared space" refers to collaboration like planning, making love, and working together. All couples establish spatial patterns whether they realize it or not. No two individuals have perfectly matched needs for privacy and togetherness. In fact, what one person defines as "togetherness" may be experienced by the other as isolation.

"Sure, we watched television together," says Paul. "But Chris sat there knitting and I felt lonely. It was like watching the program by myself."

"I felt I was with *you*," bristles Chris. "What more do you want?"

Paul yearns for a higher degree of intimacy and emotional exchange. Simply *sitting* while Chris knits isn't enough. Chris, on the other hand, is comforted by the simplicity of quietly knitting while watching a show with Paul.

Issues of psychic space are often expressed in terms of physical space. One partner needs a study of her own. The other prefers to pay the bills at the dining room table. One partner happily shares her radio, mail, and desk supplies. The other is fiercely territorial about personal property. The psychic and physical boundaries with which we feel comfortable derive from our upbringing and personal style. Let me demonstrate how couples complement each other in counterproductive ways by having rigidly matched spatial needs.

At one extreme are couples who wish to *be together, think together,* and *share together* almost all the time. Partners in a "merged" couple will find themselves reading each other's thoughts, answering questions for the other, stumbling to make mutual decisions alone, and objecting if the other takes a different stand.

"What do you want to do tonight?" asks Feliz.

"I don't know. What do *you* want to do?" Fred answers.

"I can't decide," responds Feliz. "Let's do what *you* want."

"But I don't know what I want . . . so *you* decide."

Unable to decide on anything, Feliz and Fred stay home, grow bored, and go to bed early.

When one member of a "merged" couple starts therapy, his or her partner will feel disoriented. In therapy, Feliz begins to think her own thoughts. How will Fred react to this change?

At the other end of the spectrum are partnerships in which each individual is fiercely independent. Each seeks the other out for emotional refueling. Respectful of differences, hard-driving, and self-directed, these partners 'check in' with each other to communicate where they will each be going next—separately. They are wonderfully satisfied with each other's solo activities. This balance in the relationship can shift when one of the partners—perhaps through therapy—begins to yearn for more holding, more comforting, or more time together.

"I'll be at class on Monday, giving a talk on Wednesday, and will bring my students to the house on Friday," reports Inez as usual on a Sunday night. "What will you be doing this week, Ira?"

Silence.

"Ira, I asked what you will be doing this week."

"Well," confesses Ira, "I had this idea that we might go dancing at that place in the mall on Friday."

"Since when have we gone *dancing*?" snaps Inez.

"Just a thought," apologizes Ira, feeling silly for expressing such a 'sappy' idea.

Accomplishing daily household tasks becomes a thorny problem for autonomy-bound couples. Each person is so protective of his or her time that daily chores must be regulated according to a system.

"I unloaded the dishwasher last night," protests Inez. "So it's your turn tonight!"

"But I took out the trash and folded the laundry," objects Ira in an effort to defend himself.

"Taking out the trash doesn't take as much time as unloading the dishwasher!"

"I folded the laundry, too!" Ira reminds her.

"That was *your* laundry you folded! I still had mine to fold. Perhaps we should make a chart!"

Ira and Inez resort to a scorecard mentality when shared tasks must be completed. Lacking natural instincts for cooperation, neither partner "picks up the slack" when the other is under stress. Fair is fair! Equal is equal!

Although these examples may seem extreme, they show that when couples develop established patterns skewed towards merger or separateness, changes in one individual will affect the overall relationship. If a previously dependent, stay-at-home person begins to show passion for the broader world, his or her partner may equate this change with abandonment. If a partnership is based on mutually enjoyed independence, one individual's request for "support" or companionship forces the other to recoil. Because changes of these types are common when one partner is in therapy, the "non-therapied" mate may eventually, and wisely, initiate new activities, including personal therapy. Because changes in one partner inevitably affect the entire relationship, committed partners may also seek couples therapy to help them adjust to the rearranged relationship.

Issues of independence and shared time are the constant dance of people who live together. When habitually dysfunctional patterns are disrupted, the more static partner protests vehemently. Even though therapy should address personal habits that are counter-productive, rearranged relationships teeter nervously when change is in the air.

Ideally, both parties will eventually benefit from the energy released when old inhibitions and dysfunctions dissolve. Being aware of this shift in spatial patterns is central to tolerating the disruption introduced by therapy. New differences need not spell danger if both members of the couple address relationship changes openly. Is being in therapy an excuse for neglecting a supportive partner's needs? Is knowing that a companion is in therapy a justification for burying one's own wishes?

"Stop the ship, I want to jump off!" some clients cry out. Wishing that life and all its demands could cease for a while, they want to focus solely on the therapy process and mend. However, by living fully within one's current relationship, we obtain substantive data—or "grist"—for review. We cannot do the work of therapy in a vacuum. Some people define mental health as the ability to adjust to the constantly changing demands of life. It would be countertherapeutic to "stop the ship." If you, as a partner, feel you've been dumped overboard, you will want to address this issue with your spouse. You may also want to consider couples treatment or personal therapy for yourself.

In the following pages you will read some outcries from

partners of people in therapy. You may be able to relate to one or more of their responses.

PARTNERS OF PEOPLE IN THERAPY: A FORGOTTEN POPULATION?

"She's in Another World"

If your partner is focused on self-mastery through insight-oriented therapy, his or her mind will be processing and reworking many subtle and complex ideas. Your partner may, in fact, appear to be "off in another world." Describing this process of change to a loved one not in therapy is difficult.

First, prolonged periods of confusion precede insight and clarity. People have difficulty defining their thoughts when they're confused. In sifting through the contrasting emotions that were experienced during a therapy hour, clients often proceed through a kind of incubation period. Nothing feels clear. A problem may have been identified—but painful feelings may have surfaced along with it.

Second, intense concentration is required for focusing on new sets of ideas and feelings. Time and space are needed to process new concepts. The resulting "preoccupation" of a partner in therapy is similar to many everyday demands for quiet reflection.

"Don't talk to me while I'm putting together this new recipe," says a mother to her children. She needs to concentrate in order to assure she doesn't miss a step or measure incorrectly.

"Please turn down the noise until I finish this equation," says a wife as she focuses on a physics formula. She is in a process of ordering and organizing ideas until the complex steps are distilled into one refined number. This is the work of concentration.

Therapy, like studying for an exam, requires high degrees of deliberation. Successful therapists require that *most* of the thinking and exploring occur outside the treatment hour. Clients who expect revolutionary transformations to evolve from fifty minutes are routinely disappointed. The therapy hour triggers a process that continues between appointments.

The "process" of therapy is similar to painting, poetry writing, or musical composition. New themes or melodies may surface "out of nowhere" during a walk in the woods or in sleep. The person who is progressing in therapy may, indeed, be absorbed by thoughts that are seemingly unrelated to the activities of the moment. This is his or her work. Whereas some people talk a great deal about what they are experiencing, others need time for private reflection. This doesn't mean that the people of one's current life become less life-giving. But it does imply that a highly creative project is in process.

Are you partnered to a person in therapy who seems "off in another world?" If so, you may feel left out—especially if your relationship has been of the merged sort. You can no longer "read" your partner's thoughts, nor are you invited to. Under these conditions, partners have a number of choices. They may request information or explanation. They may feel wounded and self-pitying, and withdraw from the partner in therapy. Or they may use this time to initiate new projects of their own.

"I Know She's Trying, but I'm Bored by All This Therapy Talk"

Jan and Zeke have always enjoyed the theater. Before Jan grew depressed, they would read plays together, discuss the productions they attended, and hold play-reading parties at home. Since Jan has been in treatment, it seems to Zeke that "all she talks about is 'therapy.'"

"What did you think of Macbeth's final speech after Lady Macbeth was killed?" asks Zeke on the way home from the theater.

"It reminded me of a dream I had two nights ago: 'Rage, rage against the night!' Macbeth's desperation, remorse, and total misery are like my own. My therapist thinks I react to crises in dramatic ways in order to avoid my grief," responds Jan.

"Good lord!" murmured Zeke. "Can't we ever get away from your therapist and your *issues*?"

Boredom is often a cover for irritation. Explore your reactions the next time you feel *bored* by your partner's therapy preoccupation. If you feel more irritated than "bored," ask yourself why. Do you miss the old times when your partner was more emotionally available? Are you jealous of the therapist's power and influence? Are you lonely?

This is *not* to say that a person can't be legitimately bored in terms of intellectual understimulation. Indeed, a partner in therapy may start sounding like a cracked record. Cracked records irritate us because the flow of music has been interrupted and a whining sound substituted. People jump to the stereo to turn the record off. The natural response to a partner in therapy is to want to turn off the sound—"My therapist says that . . ." "I feel angry because my therapist said . . ." "My reactions to my boss feel like . . ." "Don't talk to me like that; you sound like my mother!"

Your need for stimulation and variety will not be met if all your partner can talk about is therapy! Nor would all your needs be met if your partner talked obsessively about career matters, baseball, or a soap opera.

It is not really your partner's "therapy" that consumes him or her but rather a new, emotionally rich epic that is slowly evolving. Can you try to take an interest in the developing drama?

If you are truly irritated by your partner's repetitive preoccupations, address the concern directly. Do not be afraid that he or she is too fragile to know that you sometimes feel restless, bored, or left out. Do not be afraid that private thoughts will never be shared again. Do not be afraid of hurting your partner's feelings.

As with any adult activity requiring concentration and focus, the work of successful therapy requires energy. You will be responding countertherapeutically if you decide that you can never be direct about your own wishes. As long as you demonstrate respect for the therapeutic process and remain sensitive to your partner's vulnerabilities, you have the right to expect adequate attention for your interests and feelings. In fact, attention to you is important for *both* of you. Mental well-being is a marvelous accomplishment and gift. So, too, is a rich and open partnership. One does not need to be sacrificed for the other.

"He's Spending All His Time on Therapy But I Don't See Any Improvement"

Coleen has initiated treatment—at the suggestion of her husband—because she has become sexually dysfunctional. John expects that within several months they will be able to enjoy an active sexual relationship again. However, after four months of therapy, Coleen continues to lack desire, is tired at bedtime, is anxious and constantly worried.

John is furious and frustrated.

"I sure hope you're talking about our sexual problems with your therapist," he complains.

"Don't tell me what to talk about in therapy!" shouts Coleen. The bedside light goes out. John and Coleen thrash about in hurt, angry silence.

John thinks: I have a right to know what she's talking about with her therapist. I'm helping to pay the bills and I need to know that she's working on the problems that were bothering us. She hasn't improved a bit.

Coleen thinks: If only John could understand that I don't

want sex because it *scares* me. I don't know why sex scares me, but a lot of things scare me, like giving speeches and traveling alone. It's not as simple as he thinks. My therapy is my business. I sure hope he doesn't have an affair before I get better.

John and Coleen are suffering in different ways and for different reasons. Ideally, they would be sharing their thoughts with each other. Right now, they are too hurt, angry, and self-protective to talk.

Some problems—such as the depression that follows a job lay-off—are relatively obvious and easy to resolve. Many other symptoms require time before quantifiable results become apparent. If a person in therapy feels pressured to produce tangible "improvement," the natural pace of therapy is interrupted and resentments build. If one partner expects a specific type of outcome and resents the slow pace, the partner in treatment will protest that he or she is a person—not an object like a car which, with a tune-up, will run like new again.

If you are the partner of someone in therapy, you must be clear about several facts.

First, it is the responsibility of your partner, once in treatment, to decide with the clinician which issues will be addressed, and in what order.

Second, you cannot expect to see pre-determined "results" at a pre-determined time.

Third, "presenting problems"—or the issues that motivate a person to enter therapy—are often not the core difficulty and may be indicative of more serious underlying issues, which are rarely addressed in isolation. Unless your partner is working with a behavioral therapist, isolated symptoms become only part of the broader working picture. In Coleen's case, for example, an underlying fear of abandonment combined with guilt about sexual impulses and assertiveness are deeply embedded in her generalized timidity. Sexual dysfunction is simply one of many signs of these underlying conflicts.

Fourth, the amount of time needed for a resolution of symptoms is related to the depth and complexity of the underlying issues, your partner's capacities as a "patient," and the quality of your home environment. There is no way to predict what will happen when.

Fifth, problems or symptoms that are displayed by your partner—who has become labeled the "identified patient"—may be partially expressive of your personality and conflicts. You might want to read Maggie Scarff's book *Intimate Partners*, which discusses the concept of interlocking personality traits within a relationship. If you want to explore whether your own characteristics contribute to your spouse's problems, you may consider starting couples therapy or schedule a clinical consultation for yourself.

An appointment with a clinician will often prove relieving and revealing to the disappointed partner of someone in therapy. You might explain to the clinician that what you perceived as "his" or "her" problem is now creating difficulties for you. Say that you tried to be supportive but now you are furious. Lay out your criticism of your partner's therapist for not completing the "assignment." Explain that you are disappointed by your own irritation and diminishing resilience.

There are few—if any—relationships as complex as that of the married or deeply committed partnership. Under the best conditions long-term relationships require patience, respect, cooperation, and mutual openness about personal limits and vulnerabilities. Enduring relationships tolerate anger and disappointment as well as love. Successful relationships demand thought, compromise, sacrifice, and "work." This is why people celebrate themselves with anniversaries. The more years shared and endured together, the more there is to celebrate!

Sharing life with a vulnerable, preoccupied mate is a major test for the most supportive partner. If your loved one's early years or genetic makeup result in symptoms which compromise your quality of life, you deserve abundant support. You may need specific information about your partner's particular problem. A professional can suggest ways in which you can survive (and thrive) while helping your loved one.

Many partners of seriously depressed or symptomatic companions seek counsel or couples therapy. No matter how patient and loving you may be, you, too, have limits. Sometimes relationship crises—including affairs and angry fights—occur when partners hesitate to discuss their wishes and limitations.

"But I thought she'd love me, no matter what." wept Cory, a depressed young man in therapy. He had just learned that his wife had been having an affair.

"She's just not the *type* that has affairs!" he protested in angry despair.

His therapist asked whether his wife had been expressing how lonely she had become during his months of withdrawn isolation.

"Not once!" responded Cory. "I had no idea! If only she'd told me, I would have been more attentive."

If you are the partner of a vulnerable person, you will need to make adjustments. It's painful to admit that a partner of choice isn't as perfect and happy as you had first thought. Facing the emotional realities of a partner's serious difficulties can lead to negative reactions like denial, dismay, outrage, and grief. Or, you may decide to act positively and shoulder some of the sorrow your partner has till now carried alone through life. In this case, be sure to find mechanisms to sustain your own personal growth and refortification. Explore your options. Decide whether and how to share your loved one's burdens. Acknowledge your own needs and state them gently to your partner. Keep talking! Plan quiet time for shared experiences. Take care of yourself! These are *your* tasks while your partner is in therapy.

If your partner is receiving high quality assistance, you can assume that his or her pain—and thus yours—will diminish with time. Therapy requires sacrifice for all involved. Many believe that quality therapy is the most worthwhile investment a partnership can make.

"When She Laughs, I Think She's Healthier Than I Am!"

Emotional suffering affects both members of a couple. To the surprise of many, after therapy has been completed and the hoped-for changes are obvious, new modifications may yet be required within the relationship. Although you, as the partner, have tried in the past not to view your companion as "sick" or "fragile," you may be taken off guard by the new vitality resounding through the house.

Brenda's depression has lifted. Having released the energy that had been trapped by her depression, she's begun to exercise, seek promotions, talk about having more children—and frequently initiates sex.

"I can't keep up with you," mumbles Nick. "It's as if you've got all the energy—and I'm worn out."

Do not underestimate the surprises that can occur when your partner in therapy starts showing dramatic signs of well-being. Although changes in therapy occur slowly, the shift to vitality requires new adjustments. When Brenda had been accepted as the sick, sad, needy, and helpless one, Nick had been the strong, confident protector. Although he had made many sacrifices for her improvement, Nick hasn't yet adjusted to a "more than healthy" wife. She no longer needs him to provide solace. As her internal burdens have lifted, Nick feels vaguely depressed. What has happened to Nick?

Nick hasn't had time to catch up. Besides worrying about Brenda while she was in therapy, he had worked long hours and did more than his share at home. His role in the family, even though it had been a difficult one, had become fixed and unchanging. During Brenda's years of therapy, he had been patient and undemanding. He had listened attentively and never been intrusive. He had been conscientious about his duties as a husband. What he had neglected was his capacity to understand *himself*.

In the meantime, Brenda had had plenty of time to move through the various stages of her therapy. She had learned to monitor her feelings, make sense of her childhood, and to love herself despite her weaknesses. She had learned to laugh. Constantly in dialogue with her therapist, she had had a caring person to talk with on a regular basis. While Nick had been coping alone, Brenda had plenty of time to complete her therapy gradually.

At this stage, Nick hasn't adapted to the changes. Unaware of how much his lifestyle and identity had been influenced by Brenda's clinical depression, he was unnerved by her therapeutic success.

Nick stands back, worn out from the four year struggle. He looks at his happy, pretty wife. "Is this for real?" he asks himself. He sits down in his big leather chair as if he'd run a long distance marathon. "I'm tired," he says.

"Let's go to the movies!" responds Brenda. She hums happily while scanning the movie schedule in the paper.

"I'm just too tired," answers Nick as he dozes off.

Brenda and Nick need time to revise their lives. They must learn to play together. This is *their* task.

UNSUNG HEROES

Partners like Nick are the unsung heroes behind the people who—through hard work and courage—recover from deeply internalized, chronic pain. The people who arrive at a therapist's office usually know that their sorrows have become the sorrows of their loved ones. They seek comfort for themselves and also for their loved ones from whom they feel so alienated. Many people in therapy, torn by internal conflict, know that their capacities for loving have been damaged. They are aware that they have lost the ability to love themselves, their partners, their families and friends. Feeling empty, they sometimes wonder whether they ever really loved at all. Wanting to look outward instead of inward, they need encouragement to look both ways. For them and their partners, this self-review represents sacrifice.

As stated by a married urban planner as he initiated therapy:

"I don't like thinking about myself. It's not like me to be so self-absorbed. I've grown bitter. I want to be able to love again. I hope my wife will wait for me. If I don't do this therapy, I'll lose her for sure." Zachary bowed his head and wept. "I've worn my wife out with my self-pity. I hope she won't give up on me."

Sometimes partners of unhappy people do give up. Fatigued by the pressures imposed by companions who complain about life while creating misery for others, they seek the refuge of individuals whose affection is less demanding. Many partners, on the other hand, have full confidence in their loved ones' capacities to resolve their problems. Vividly recalling the qualities that were so appealing in their partners, they maintain a deep conviction about the inherent goodness of their loved ones. These are partners who know that loving is hard work. "Loving" means "loving actions." Supportive partners are the unsung heroes of our therapy hours.

We, as therapists, hear about those of you who stay up at night listening to those we treat by day. We hear of the encouragement and insights you offer your partners. We hear of those who challenge, comfort, and confront with intelligence and sensitivity. Although we may never meet you, we feel reassured when we know that our clients are not suffering alone. To those of you who love enough to offer needed support, we therapists are grateful.

Although each of us must walk this lonesome valley by ourselves, it is reassuring to know that some are walking through it together.

CHAPTER 10

"AM I
MY BROTHER'S
KEEPER?"

"No more problems!" wept Danielle, whose sister had started hallucinating after experimenting with drugs. "I took care of my drunken father—I will *not* take care of my sister, too!"

Whether or not you choose to be your brother or sister's keeper, you probably feel concern for a sibling, relative, or friend with serious problems. People react in different ways to peers who are in therapy. If you have a sibling or peer in treatment, your respones to their problems and therapy processes will be different from those of parents or partners.

A *friend* may tell you more about the problems that precipitated therapy than he or she would tell a parent. Your peer may feel that he or she doesn't need to protect you from painful truths that would be hurtful to family members. An unhappy friend may assume that you will be more objective and non-judgmental and that you will endorse his or her feelings as valid. Unlike a family member, you will probably feel freer to engage and disengage yourself from your friend's crises and intrusions.

If you are the *sibling* of someone with serious problems, you will face different issues from those of a parent or friend. You won't suffer parental guilt but you may still feel a responsibility for your brother's or sister's distress and feel impelled to come to the rescue. People often underestimate the intense ties that bind brothers and sisters. Old jealousies, rivalries, and competitive struggles are mixed with high degrees of mutual understanding and loyalty. Your sibs were your first playmates. As co-observer of parental and family dynamics, you are able to understand your sibling's childhood more completely than anyone else and so be helpful when your sib goes into therapy. "After all," said an inner city police officer who was housing his sibling Tony, a victim of schizophrenia, "he's my brother. I want to take care of him."

On the other hand, if a sister or brother is deeply disturbed and unpleasant to be with, you may not want extra burdens or the reminders of hard times.

THE EXTENDED FAMILY OF ADULT PEERS

Close friends often grow to feel like brothers and sisters. In such relationships, friends sometimes "parent" each other—receiving from their bond what was once yearned for from parents. People often extinguish the mismatching within their original families when choosing friends. While in childhood we can't select our parents, aunts and uncles, in adulthood we can control who "our people" will be. We select friends with matching or complementary temperaments, comparable values, and similar interests. Once selected, friends form our expanded family.

The ways in which we care for peers are matters of personal style, personal limitation, and personal choice. We all have problems, some minor, such as car trouble, and some major, such as the loss of a parent. Individuals move through life's challenges with varying degrees of effort. Some of us are resilient and strong while others are delicate and suffer greatly. Some of those who suffer psychic pain may seek therapy.

The work of therapy or any individualized treatment program requires discipline, focus, and emotional engagement with a clinician. Therapists are heartened when they learn that a new client has friendship networks. If you are a member of that network, you may notice that your relationship with your friend has changed, sometimes for the better, sometimes for the worse. The following types of comments and questions arise in the minds of peers who care about a friend in therapy.

Some Questions and Thoughts of Parenting Peers

Asks her sister: "I know it's not my fault that mother preferred me over Paula, but I feel guilty about her poor self-image. Am I to blame?"

Wonders his older brother: I know I'm not his therapist, but I feel responsible for Charlie. He's depressed and I don't know whether he's suicidal. Should he live with me for awhile?

As stated by Pam's friend: "All Pam talks about is her therapy and therapist. I'm tired of this but, I feel I should be interested. I feel I've lost my best friend."

Scott's baseball buddy reflects: "Scott's drinking bouts are becoming more frequent. His therapist doesn't know about his alcoholism. Should I call the therapist to advise her of the addiction?"

As pondered by a hiking companion: Bernice has a super therapist. I wonder if I could work with a therapist, too.

States Randall's frequent date: "I feel trapped by Randy's depression. I've wanted to pull out of the relationship for a long time. Knowing how fragile he is, I'm scared he might kill himself if I let him know."

Ramon's sister is upset: "Ramon is always calling me in distress. I want to help him but I don't have time to chat each night. Should I tell him to call his therapist instead?"

Asks his brother: "Caleb has been in treatment for four

years. He says he likes his therapist even though the therapist forgets appointments and is usually late. I think Caleb should find another therapist. Should I pressure him to change?"

THE VALUE OF BEING DIRECT

None of the questions have simple answers. Each conveys a level of involvement between a person in therapy and a concerned friend or sibling. As we review these concerns, I will emphasize the importance of direct communication between you and your peers. Therapy—as an undertaking—is no more distinct from normal daily life than any other project. The therapy process has its own set of conventions and restrictions. Direct communication between friends or siblings is very important.

Relationships become imbalanced if one person is viewed as "weak" while the other is "strong." People coming to therapy must learn to love and respect themselves and others for who they are. Love is good medicine and is best when used wisely.

BIG PROBLEMS, SMALL PROBLEMS

"Who's to Blame?"

Siblings may wonder why their sisters and brothers are not thriving. Knowing too much or too little, they often claim responsibility for problems that are not of their making.

Priscilla and Paula

Priscilla knows that she is not responsible for Paula's poor self-image. It is true that they were competitive as children and that Priscilla received more praise than did Paula. Priscilla would often tease Paula, as older sisters sometimes do. Now an adult, Priscilla feels uncomfortable about her sister's depression. Intellectually, she knows it's not her fault that Paula's self-esteem is fragile. However, as her sister's condition has led to emotional withdrawal and angry outbursts at "pretty Priscilla," Priscilla grows concerned that she is the cause of Paula's problems. Priscilla doesn't know whether her efforts to help Paula would be appreciated. She wonders whether Paula's therapist is encouraging Paula's angry outbursts. Priscilla has tried to call Paula, who responds, "You always had it easy . . . and now you try to *help*?"

Feeling guilty about the times she teased Paula when they were young, Priscilla asks, "Am I to blame?"

When initiating therapy, people must claim full responsibility for solving personal problems that interfere with living. Reproaching others for one's difficulties is neither productive nor healing. Blaming and shaming are not the tools of a qualified therapist. Clients who gain mastery over their problems must own full responsibility for their recovery regardless of the precipitating causes for the distress.

Although one sibling might feel guilt about being the preferred child, it is each sibling's responsibility to deal with the consequences of early childhood injustices. Furthermore, being the "preferred" child is not always an advantage. For example, if you were the favored child of an abusive alcoholic, you may have been more deeply damaged by your parent's illness than a neglected sibling. Feeling at fault for a sibling's difficulties as Priscilla does neglects to take into account how helpless both sisters were when young. Priscilla is feeling "survivor guilt," felt by a person who suffered similar circumstances but survived instead of deteriorating.

Post script: Priscilla continued to try to reach out to Paula who continued to respond with bitter hostility. Finally, Priscilla wrote Paula a letter.

Dear Paula,

I feel that my calls to you are not welcome. Have I done something to offend you? I know you're having a hard time and I don't want to complicate your life. I'm glad you're in therapy. I think we both had a hard time as kids . . . with Mom's drinking problems and Dad's anger. You have a lot to offer. Please know that I'm here for you, but I won't keep calling you. Please call me if and when you want to talk.

Love,
Priscilla

During the course of her therapy, Paula learned that her rage at her mother, a depressed alcoholic, had been displaced onto her sister who had served as a substitute caretaker. Paula needed to do *something* with her anger, so Priscilla became the target. This was actually a clever stratagem since her mother would get drunk when people criticized her. As she explored the sources of her anger, Paula also learned that she had idealized Priscilla who had been pretty and kindly. In trying to become psychologically separate from big "sis," she had pushed her away. As Paula became more self-loving and less angry about her chaotic childhood, she re-established her relationship with Priscilla. Their relationship is now gratifying to both.

"Is He Suicidal?"

Charlie worries that his younger brother is suicidal. His brother Jay lives alone. Depressed since the death of their father, Jay has withdrawn from previously enjoyed activities, has begun to drink, and makes occasional references to wanting to "end it all." Charlie knows that Jay was a sensitive child and especially attached to their father. It was Charlie's job to watch out for "little Jay." Charlie is not sure whether Jay is suicidal, how to help, or whether he should call Jay's therapist.

If you're wondering whether a partner, friend or relative is suicidal, your concern itself is an important signal. There is one rule of thumb about suicidal threats or implications: *Take them seriously!* It is better to err on the side of safety than to overlook what might be a hesitant or unconscious call for rescue. This is one time when phoning the therapist is indicated. Suicidal individuals should not be living alone. If your friend or relative has become isolated, sees no reason to live, and mentions that he or she has *not* told the therapist of suicidal thoughts, you have reason to be very concerned. This person may need to attend more frequent therapy sessions, agree to temporary hospitalization, or review medication options. If at-risk peers refuse to call therapists, you can assist them by calling the clinician yourself. Just ask for the therapist's phone number and calmly mention that you want to talk with him or her. This is one of those rare occasions when your direct involvement in the treatment process can be life-saving. Of course, if your friend is actively suicidal, call the emergency number 911, or drive him or her directly to the hospital. Individuals with strong support networks are less likely to attempt suicide than those who live alone and remove themselves from peer relationships.

"Should I Tell Her I'm Tired of Hearing About Therapy?"

"You talk as though you're in *love* with your therapist," Jill said resentfully. She leaned over to decorate the last Christmas cookie.

"Well, I *am* in love with him," responded Pam dreamily as she sprinkled sugar on a holiday tart. "I think about him day and night. I dream about him. It's wonderful."

Good grief, thinks Jill. Is this what you pay a hundred dollars a visit for? You can get a boyfriend for free!

Many people are private and reserved about their therapy processes. While reviewing a recent session or new ideas, they may wear "the face of reflection" and appear to be in deep thought. Processing new connections between past and present patterns of emotion requires disciplined attention. Sometimes, after a good cry or the reliving of an old fear, your friend may appear emotionally drained. This is the work of many people in therapy. During periods of concentration, some clients speak very little about their treatment.

Others, however, may talk "therapy this" and "my therapist that" all the time. How can you, as a friend or relative, address this irritating intrusion into your relationship? You're tired of hearing about therapy! "Every time I start to talk about myself," says Pam's friend Jill, "Pam diverts the conversation back to herself and her *therapy*! I don't want to tell her I'm annoyed because I know how important her therapist is to her."

Although you may want to be responsive to the events in the life of a close friend, you are weary about hearing about a therapist you've never met. "Don't you care about *me* anymore?" Jill wants to scream, but she doesn't dare to object openly. After all, Pam has always been afraid of men and has never been in love. Jill is glad that Pam is learning to love in a safe environment. "But next year," reflects Jill, "I'll make Christmas cookies with someone else."

Jill is angry. By withholding her feelings, she is contributing to the increasing distance that is developing between herself and her closest friend. Pam, who has always been self-centered and preoccupied, might benefit from Jill's direct feedback.

Delicate Directness

Constructive communication requires direct, caring, and open exchange of feelings and ideas between people. Communication experts find that when we state simply what we think and feel about a specific situation, the listener will absorb the idea.

Therefore, Jill might say, "Pam, I'm glad you're getting a lot from your therapy. But every time I start to talk, I feel cut off by your introspections. Please listen to me, too!"

With caring "I statements" like these, our friends are more apt to listen because their characters are not globally attacked. Sensing that we value the friendship enough to address it, friends respond with gratitude, over time. If friendships fade while therapy thrives, the self-absorbed client may find his or her support network depleted by termination time.

The opposite situation occurs when the person in therapy *never* talks about the therapy. His or her friend may be curious and wants to hear about issues that are being addressed. "Bill's so private about his therapy that I don't dare to ask him what he's working on," states Bill's girlfriend. "I never know what he's thinking any more."

In insight-oriented therapy, no topics are "taboo." The client is encouraged to talk about everything and anything that comes to mind. Let your friend know that you are curious about therapy. Ask him or her to tell you what it's like. Ask if it's okay to ask! To your surprise, you may learn that your peer thought you weren't interested or would find his or her issues "silly."

"Should I Intervene About an Addiction Problem?"

Scott's old baseball partner notices that Scott is drinking more and playing ball less. By now, most of Scott's social activities revolve around alcohol. Jerry, an old high school friend, is concerned not only about the drinking but also about the fact that Scott's therapist doesn't seem to be addressing the substance abuse. Jerry wonders whether he should call the therapist to advise him of the problem and Scott's denial.

Alert to the early signs of alcoholism (and other forms of drug abuse) which include withdrawal and denial, Jerry is convinced that Scott needs active, aggressive intervention before his best friend loses his job and endangers his health. Since alcoholism can be life threatening, Scott's therapist should be advised even though he or she, trained to detect substance abuse, is probably alert to the problem. Nevertheless, friends and relatives are right to become concerned if abusive behaviors continue to accelerate. An equally relevant question, however, is whether Jerry has spoken directly to Scott about his self-destructive behaviors.

The best time to confront a partner, friend or relative about a substance problem is when he or she is sober. Confronting someone who is intoxicated is useless. Although your friend may dismiss your concerns as "ridiculous," you must insist firmly that your friend address this problem in therapy.

Mental health professionals deal with addiction problems in different ways. Once a meaningful attachment has been formed between clinician and client, the professional is in a favorable position to actively address the self-abusive behavior. If your peer reports that his or her therapist doesn't talk much about the alcohol problem, the therapist may be waiting until a strong enough bond has been formed to assure a productive dialogue. Without a strong therapeutic alliance, an addicted client may bolt from treatment if the substance abuse is targeted too soon.

Clinicians challenge their addicted patients with direct, concerned honesty. Helping a client crack through his or her terror and denial may take a long time. Once abstinence is acquired, the true processes of recovery and insight-oriented therapy can be initiated.

Alcohol and drugs sabotage the treatment process. Clients who try to hide the severity of their habits are putting more energy into the substance than into the therapy. For this reason, many clinicians insist that sobriety be maintained before other therapeutic issues can be addressed.

If your friend or relative is working with an addictions specialist, the addictive behaviors may be the primary focus of the therapeutic work. The client may have been referred by the judge because of driving while drinking. His or her employer, lover, or spouse may have demanded that the problem be rectified. In these cases, the patient needs a prolonged period to claim responsibility for the problem. After all, someone else "sent" him or her for treatment! A personal desire for recovery is essential for a successful outcome. For this reason, some substance abusers do not face their addictive behaviors until they are middle-aged, financially destitute, and physically compromised. By then they can no longer deny the cause for their self-induced plight. Emotionally desperate, they are finally able to admit that they have a problem.

With the caring concern of friends, relatives, and skilled professionals, many people with addiction problems are now receiving help at younger ages. Groups such as Alanon welcome concerned relatives and peers who seek information about alcoholism and addiction.

Some "self-medicators" initiate therapy because others (usually the court or a spouse) have insisted upon treatment. Many other adults initiate psychotherapy on their own. Depressed and anxious, they have grown concerned about the drugs they are consuming to soothe psychic pain. Many clinicians launch treatment by explaining that the abused substance represents a form of self-medication. Despite their anxiety, these clients may avoid discussing the addiction problem for a long time. Too scared to relinquish their only source of comfort but informed enough to know that recovery requires suffering, these sensitive people live in fear.

Although your friend or relative may be outraged and insulted by your "intrusiveness," your open, informed confrontation of the addiction is the most caring gift you can offer. You are colluding with a dangerous habit unless you speak directly with your friend. Try to be firm, caring, and non-judgmental. Stress that addiction is a life-threatening illness that is treatable. The earlier an abuse problem is accepted by the addicted person, the less difficult the recovery process will be. You have reason to worry if your peer's therapist is truly unaware of his or her substance abuse.

If you have not confronted your friend directly about your concerns, you must ask yourself "Why not?" Are you afraid of your peer's angry withdrawal, denial, or rejection? If so, you are more likely to sustain this valued relationship if you address your fears for his or her health clearly. Be persistent.

You are watching a friend walk into the street as a giant delivery truck veers around the corner. As you watch your buddy proceed unaware toward the truck, won't you shout "Stop?"

"Can I Start Therapy with My Best Friend's Therapist?"

Bernice, while hiking with Katrina, speaks with excitement about her therapist. "She's warm, she's funny, and she's smart," states Bernice as they pull themselves up the rocky slope.

"She sounds super," puffs Katrina. "Would it be okay if I made an appointment to see her, too?"

Bernice stops walking. She grows flushed. Looking at Katrina she shouts, "In no way are you going to work with my therapist!"

"Just a question," mutters Katrina. She is stunned.

Katrina's shocked confusion is understandable. She is unaware of the delicacy of some people's issues. Bernice, for example, was the third of four sisters. When she was born, her parents had hoped for a son. She was viewed as the family's "ugly duckling." Her mother often apologized to others about

Bernice's glasses, her freckles, and her crooked teeth. Although Bernice has become both physically beautiful and emotionally charming, she still needs to protect her singular relationship with her therapist. Having felt neglected as a child, she cannot tolerate the thought that her therapist would prefer her best friend—as her mother had preferred her older sisters—over her. She needs time to feel special and valuable in a protected relationship.

Katrina, on the other hand, was the long-awaited daughter whose birth was celebrated with parental joy. As the favored child in a family with five boys, she is unable to relate to the pain of feeling "second best." Although Katrina has other issues (notably fear of success) which motivate her interest in therapy, she *assumes* that people will accept and enjoy her. She rarely feels threatened when she shares her friends. She might even be glad to refer a close friend to her therapist.

Do psychotherapists work with the close friends and relatives of a client in treatment? Mental health professionals work in varied ways. Some clinicians are willing to work individually with the friends and relations of a client. Other therapists insist that, in order to safeguard the working alliance with a patient, loved ones must be referred elsewhere. If you call to make an appointment with a professional who inquires as to who referred you, he or she is assessing whether the referring individual is currently in his or her care. Although the referring client might not foresee difficulties that could arise in both the friendship and therapy, the therapist will refer you to a colleague to safeguard the therapy process of your friend or relative.

Mental health professionals make these determinations based on their varying theory bases, their technical and personal styles, and the availability of other qualified clinicians. A skilled clinician will *always* keep the interests of his or her current patients in mind when initiating treatment with a new person.

In small towns with only one or two therapists, local residents typically share the same clinicians, with good results. The same psychologist may be seeing four individuals who live on the same street. Being the only therapist in town, she must hold to high standards of confidentiality and commitment to all her clients. If people who "share" therapists can talk openly with their clinicians about the competitive, jealous, or hurt feelings that may arise, deep-seated relationship problems may be explored and corrected within the local setting.

As clinicians, we do our best to preserve the well-being of our clients. Some mental health facilities stand in public view. Others are hidden in private locations where no one would know that you are seeing a therapist. In large cities, a person seeking therapy may choose among hundreds of qualified professionals, as opposed to the one practitioner in a small town. The only essential is that the professional you select is highly trained, ethical, and emotionally stable. Do not work with a therapist who is casual about confidentiality.

Postscript: Bernice described to her therapist her rage at Katrina. Katrina's innocent question had reactivated Bernice's repressed anger about her prettier, preferred sisters. She was able to review her childhood neglect and shame within the new, corrective relationship. Her therapist stated that it would be countertherapeutic for Bernice to "share" her therapist with Katrina. She did, however, offer the phone numbers of other clinicians. Katrina is now working with someone else, and her friendship with Bernice continues to thrive. More adventuresome in their hiking than ever before, they are also exploring the canyons and peaks of their separate identities.

"I Feel Trapped by My Lover's Depression, But Don't Dare to Break Up"

Randall had become clinically depressed while in a

romantic relationship with Rene. Rene is not in love with Randall and has wanted to leave the relationship for six months. Randy spends his days in bed and speaks of wanting to die. Whenever Rene refers to a possible breakup, Randy insists that he will "kill himself" if she abandons him.

Rene, who is conscientious, feels trapped. Although miserable with Randy, she could not tolerate her own guilt if Randy went ahead and killed himself. How can she know whether Randall's suicidal threats are serious? What are her options?

Although this may seem to be an extreme example of the gripping bind that friends of depressed people feel, it is a common problem. The "depression trap" takes many forms.

Sometimes peers decide they should never express anger, irritation, or any sign of disapproval towards a depressed friend or relative. Sensitive to the depressed person's extreme fragility, peers tiptoe in constant fear of another depressive episode.

The Faces of Depression

Twenty percent of all people suffer from depression. There are many types of the illness. "Major depressions" include disorders manifesting symptoms such as sleeplessness or weight loss, suicidal preoccupation, hopelessness, a sense of worthlessness, and lost enthusiasm. People suffering from less severe forms of depression (dysthymia, for example) may display similar symptoms which are less intense, less frequent, and of shorter duration. Feelings of worthlessness and helplessness are common in depression victims.

Other individuals may experience depressed, unhappy moods after a major life transition. For them, depression may be combined with feelings like anxiety and fear. As these individuals recover after the precipitating crisis (such as a divorce), the depression typically abates. These people are suffering from an "adjustment disorder" which includes periods of understand-able depressed mood.

Because depression has so many faces and carries so many connotations, it is difficult for a lover, friend, or relative to assess how serious the condition really is. People like Rene feel obligated to friends who are depressed. They are aware of the fragility, sensitivity to loss, and dangers inherent to depression. They feel especially responsible if the depressed person lacks support networks and threatens self harm if certain conditions are not met.

As stated earlier, suicidal threats or references must be taken *very* seriously. If you are feeling the sole responsibility for the life and safety of a friend, you need assistance. Unless this crisis requires emergency hospitalization, you will feel relieved if you schedule a consultation with a mental health professional to discuss this potentially hazardous situation. By notifying close relatives and your friend's therapist, you will feel less alone.

Although many people remain friends through hard times, some relationships aren't inherently solid enough to handle the complex pressures of a peer's severe depression. By remaining in an unfulfilling, binding, threat-induced relationship, you may unknowingly be fostering your peer's helplessness, and you will be harming yourself as well. The longer you deny your anger and frustrations about this arrangement, the more likely you are to suddenly explode or bolt impulsively from the relationship. This could be more hazardous for your friend than a more carefully planned departure.

Should you decide to break away from an individual who is exquisitely sensitive to loss, the depressed person will need extra support from others during the transition. If therapists are aware of the situation, they may review medication options, schedule extra appointments, or, if clinically necessary, encourage supportive hospitalization until the potential crisis has passed.

Life, along with all its pleasures, is also marked with losses. We have all experienced the loss of friends, lovers, relatives, jobs, self-esteem or physical health at some point in time. To kill oneself because of a failed relationship implies an underlying vulnerability for which no one person can be held responsible.

If you know someone like Randall who implies that you alone could cause his demise, you must recognize his faulty thinking. You must also recognize that suicidal threats are often serious and demand immediate intervention. If depressed peers find protection, they can be helped. If a sibling or friend does commit suicide and you believe that your leaving caused it, please remember that you did not cause his or her underlying vulnerabilities. You can neither solve your friend's problems nor claim full responsibility for their pre-existing conditions. Be kind but clear about what you can and cannot offer. Make careful plans. Then say "goodbye" with hope-enhancing affirmations.

Depressive Helplessness

Feelings of helplessness characterize many depressed people. Instead of believing that they can solve life's problems, they become paralyzed with the psychic pain of inaction and despair. Feeling alone and dejected, depressed people believe that the darkness will never be relieved. During treatment, these individuals will probably need medication so that they can revise their assumption that solutions cannot be found.

Depression, as a clinical diagnosis, is highly responsive to therapeutic and medication interventions. If Randall claims that he is helpless and could not tolerate the pain of Rene's departure, he *must* address these issues with his therapist. When individuals display a helpless syndrome, relatives and friends often feel manipulated. They are unable to assess whether or not they are being "conned" into performing tasks which the depressed individual could really accomplish himself. Sometimes they are being manipulated, but at other times the depressed person may truly be incapable of rallying the strength required for a designated emotional challenge. These determinations must be discussed with a qualified professional.

Postscript: Rene, after advising Randall's therapist and relatives about his suicidal threats, spent several weeks conveying her concerns to Randy. She told him that although she "cared" about him, she would soon be moving to a place of her own. After Rene found another apartment, Randall was angry and grief-stricken. He learned, through his therapy, that his terror of abandonment and the pressure he had placed on Rene were primarily related to his mother's suicide when he was six. Rene's threat of departure had reactivated the terror and genuine helplessness which little Randy had felt when his mother died. Rene's sensitively planned farewell precipitated one of the most productive phases of Randall's therapeutic journey.

After several months of grief and "working through," Randy's depression began to lift. His relationships with women became more mutual and less binding. No longer haunted by helplessness, Randy was able to move on with life.

"Should I Tell Him to Call His Therapist Instead of Calling Me?"

Therapists differ in their telephone practices. Qualified therapists establish telephone backup services for major crises and life threatening emergencies. Some wear pagers; most own answering machines. If the therapist is in group practice or sees clients in a mental health facility, he or she may "share call" with colleagues. Most qualified practitioners arrange for other therapists to cover their practice when they are out of town. Clients deserve to know how their therapists may be reached in the event of a crisis.

But what constitutes a crisis?

It is the client's responsibility to discuss this question with his or her therapist. Some clinicians encourage clients to call only if all other resources have been utilized or the crisis is life threatening. Not wanting to deter the client's efforts to develop meaningful support networks, these therapists want to convey availability without fostering exclusive dependency on the therapist.

Other practitioners believe in the therapeutic value of being easily accessible when crises are related to therapeutic issues currently being discussed. These clinicians feel that problems such as an impending anxiety attack or the fear of an alcoholic "slip" merit a brief call. They would prefer to be in touch with a client between sessions rather than learn a week later that the client had suffered an emotional relapse. Most therapists believe that people benefit from putting their problems into words instead of "acting out" their feelings. For example, if a client is learning to harness impulsively angry outbursts while on the job or parenting young children, he or she may be urged to call the therapist and *talk* about anger before losing control. Therapists encourage some of their clients to call them on a regular basis whereas this encouragement may not be necessary for others.

The "hows" and "whens" of calling the therapist should be discussed during the treatment hour. Some people, once invited to phone the therapist, want to call every day. Others with life-long fears of bothering people refuse to call even when a ten-minute talk is indicated.

Since knowing whether or not to call the therapist is often a complex decision for clients, it is even more confusing for the peer or relative who has not received guidelines about telephone usage. Potentially life-threatening episodes are definite occasions when the therapist and relatives must be called immediately.

Ramon

Ramon calls his sister Gwen two or three times a day. As he drives home from work, he passes by her apartment building to see whether her lights are on yet. He usually calls to ask her advice on personal issues, to tell her how distressed he is, or to discuss his upsets with his therapist or his boss. Ramon needs to talk.

By now, Gwen, who was initially excited when her younger brother started therapy, is tired of his calls. She grows tense when the phone rings and wants to buy an answering machine to screen his calls. Not wanting to abandon or hurt Ramon, she has not told him directly that the frequency of his calls is irritating her. Not knowing how to handle Ramon's invasiveness, Gwen tells him to call his therapist instead of her.

Ramon's support network consists of his sister and therapist. Socially isolated, he has never had a group of friends. Without thinking, Ramon assumes that Gwen—who always served as a mother figure—wants to hear about his problems.

Just as Ramon needs to learn about Gwen's limitations, Gwen must learn to set loving limits. If Ramon were to call his therapist every night, he would be asked to save his concerns for the therapy hour. Therapists are not "phone friends." First, it isn't feasible for therapists to talk every night with clients. Second, were clinicians to allow frequent phone chats, clients might never form lasting friendships outside of therapy.

If you are the relative or friend of someone whose constant demands become increasingly annoying, you must ask yourself why you are not confronting this problem and discussing it directly. Are you afraid to hurt another's feelings? Do you worry that by stating limits lovingly, you will never be called again? Do you need to feel needed—even though you are annoyed by the intrusions?

"She Loves Me—She Loves Me Not"

People who were raised in families where personal boundaries were not respected have difficulty setting—and accepting—loving limits. These families organize themselves around "either-or" principles: either you love me or you don't; either you're interested or you're not; either you care or you don't give a 'hoot.' People who use these equations are vulnerable to the moods of others. In seeking friends who are always available, fragile individuals often become overly dependent on their acquaintances. They often alienate the very people for whose affection they most yearn. "She loves me, she loves me not" are the only options.

Gwen didn't realize that she could lovingly explain to Ramon that since she needs her evenings to prepare for the next day, she and he will have to limit their phone time. Because of Gwen's "either-or" thinking, she has concluded that "either I talk to my brother for as long as he wants, or I don't talk at all." She fears that Ramon would conclude, "she loves me not."

Expressing limitations in gentle and caring ways safeguards valued relationships. If you accept others' limits without feeling permanently rejected, you protect yourself from unnecessary hurt. These are some common issues with which some people in therapy struggle all the time.

"Should I Suggest That He Find Another Therapist?"

Caleb's brother Jack is outraged whenever he hears about the treatment Caleb is receiving from his therapist. Caleb's doctor has forgotten five appointments this year. When they do meet, the therapist is usually twenty minutes late but charges Caleb for a full hour. Caleb reports that the doctor is often sleepy and frequently dozes during appointments.

Nevertheless, Caleb "likes" his therapist who has grown

to know him well over four years. Caleb forgives the therapist for missing sessions and dozing. "He's probably under stress," Caleb says. He objects to his older brother's criticism of his therapist. "If you just knew how *nice* he is, you'd understand," protests Caleb.

In a professional, being "nice" is not enough. Honoring historic codes of ethics and behavior are important to maintaining the high standards of mental health practitioners. All viable human relationships are based on contracts—whether they are spoken, written, or assumed. The therapeutic relationship should be a caring human contract which is taken seriously by both the therapist and the client.

The agreed-upon time for a meeting is a form of contract.

The establishment of a meeting date is a contract.

When a person decides to work with a clinician, an unwritten contract is established: the licensed professional is assumed to be well-trained, ethical and emotionally available.

If therapists routinely sabotage established contracts with clients, they must rigorously examine and repair the causes of their own violations. Similarly, clients must face the realities of broken agreements by confronting their therapists and exploring other options.

Psychotherapists are people, too. On some days they are more energetic, rested, and resourceful than on other days. Most clients are quite forgiving of their therapists' human foibles. Many outstanding therapists can recall a horrifying day when they either "double booked" two clients at the same time, wrote the wrong hour on their calendars, or—in the rush of the holiday season—went to the uptown office while a client was waiting to meet them downtown. A skilled therapist will claim full responsibility for these human errors and take time to explore how his or her mistakes affect the client. In situations such as these, therapist and client work together to resume the normal therapeutic climate.

However, because some clients form intense attachments to their therapists, they can become *too* accepting of contract violations. The thought of losing (or abandoning) the therapist may be so wrenching that some clients continue with non-therapeutic "therapy" for far too long. Vulnerable adults who are accustomed to being ignored don't even know when they are being exploited. Jack's brother Caleb, who had been seriously abused during childhood, hardly noticed his therapist's contractual breaches. After all, when the therapist did show up for scheduled appointments, he was "very nice." He never lost his temper like Caleb's father.

Ideally, Caleb would confront his therapist about his falling asleep and missing appointments, but Caleb didn't dare to offend the therapist or "make him mad." The problems which his doctor introduced to treatment hours were neither addressed nor challenged.

A number of therapeutic situations may puzzle friends, but are not indicative of unethical therapist behavior. The following examples represent situations where clients get mad or sad in a wholesome way as part of their recovery.

If your friend or sibling is angry—even outraged—at the therapist, he or she may be on the mend. When clients become trusting and expressive, their anger can be intense. Clients will try to convince friends that the clinician was uncaring, disinterested, or unfair. They may have misheard the words or intent of the therapist while recalling the innuendoes of their mother or father. At times like these, your friend is probably working through important personal issues that pre-date (and often were the reason for) treatment. A qualified therapist accepts the client's anger in order to understand its critical meaning. Unless your friend is angry about a clear breach of contract or ethics, you can assume that he or she is re-working old injuries in a new, corrective setting. This is *not* a time for your friend to retreat from treatment. You can help by asking about the hurt that lies beneath the anger. Encourage your peer to keep talking with the therapist until the angry pain has been fully expressed and understood.

If your sibling, partner, or friend returns from therapy appointments upset or in tears, you may wonder whether the therapist was hurtful, insensitive, or callous. Some therapists are confrontational when an important issue is consistently avoided by the client. Others are gentle and choose to wait until the client introduces delicate topics. Since people seek therapy because they are in pain, it is inevitable that some sessions will address the distress and evoke painful feelings. At times like these, people in therapy benefit from the support and encouragement of relatives and friends.

In Caleb's case, his core problem is displayed by his *lack* of anger or remorse regarding his therapist's breaches of contract. As in childhood, he was "numb" to his own emotions. He forgave the unacceptable and accepted the untenable status quo. Jack eventually pressured his brother to see another therapist. However, Caleb's attachment to his therapist was too intense, and he refused to leave. This was Caleb's choice. It would have been a sign of emotional maturity if Caleb had been able to confront his therapist and move on to a more reliable clinician.

Please note: If you know of therapists like Caleb's who demonstrate inadequate standards of care, call your local mental health association, a lawyer, or your state's licensing board for information about submitting formal complaints against a practitioner. State laws vary and the mechanisms for reporting complaints differ. Although therapists like this one misrepresent the profession's ethical values, far more serious is the wasted time—if not damage—rendered to vulnerable clients like Caleb who could have thrived in a more wholesome clinical setting.

"WHO'S THE KEEPER OF WHOM?"

Whether you are the brother, sister, friend, or relative of someone who chooses to grow through psychotherapy, you may find yourself indirectly affected by your peer's new pursuits. The extent to which we can serve as each other's "keepers" varies with life phase, competing responsibilities, our personalities, and the nature of the valued relationship. There is nothing mysterious about psychotherapy. Just as you are part of your peer's support network, a qualified professional will also become invested in his or her well-being. After completing therapy, most individuals are more self-accepting and caring towards their friends. By turning vulnerabilities into personal strengths, they may finally become more compassionate towards you.

Whatever you offer your friends and relatives during their "hard times" will be returned to you some day. We clinicians are in privileged positions. We hear about your sensitive and wise concern. Your gifts to your peers in therapy help us to tolerate the tragic dimensions of our work. Through our clients we learn that there are many brotherly and sisterly "keepers" beyond our office doors.

CHAPTER 11

WITH RESPECT TO SUPERVISORS, BOSSES . . . AND OTHER COLLEGIAL FOLK

It is eleven thirty-five in the morning.

Bill Jelsey, a thirty-two-year-old radiologist, rises from his office chair. He peeks through his consultation room door and peers down the hall. The administrative station is quiet. All's clear. Grabbing his lunch and his raincoat, Bill furtively scoots down the hall. He attempts to look professionally preoccupied, but his heart pounds as he hears noise in the executive office. He escapes to the elevator, breathes a sigh of relief, and refocuses his attention.

Bill is on his way to his therapy appointment.

Each week Bill arrives at his therapist's office feeling harried and anxious.

"I'd like to tell the clinic administrator where I'm going," he tells the therapist, "but I don't know what Chad would think. He might conclude that I'm emotionally disturbed. That's why I keep my appointment private."

Bill pays a price for his privacy. If he were going to physical therapy or to the gym, he could easily explain his weekly disappearances. But "therapy," he feels, has a risky ring.

Bill doesn't know what the chief radiologist would think about one of his doctors seeing a "shrink." Although the administrator may be seeing a therapist himself, Bill can't count on this nor can he know how the administrator might feel about mental health counseling.

It's sad but not surprising that many employees have to keep their therapy visits secret. The mental health histories of some professionals—politicians, for instance—are scrutinized in public. If psychotherapy or emotional difficulties become a subject of press inquiries, rumors spread fast. Michael Dukakis' mental history, for example, was questioned during his presidential campaign. In response to the rumors which were spread about Mr. Dukakis' emotional stability, Coleman McCarthy wrote:

Candor, if not full disclosure, was the choice Michael Dukakis finally made in response to rumors about his mental health. . . . From this, the public can conclude that no valium, no electroshocks, no $80.00 an hour psychotherapy and no workdays lost to depression, neurosis, or psychosis lurk in Dukakis' past. . . . The presumption in these cases when political fitness is twinned with lifelong psychological well-being is that mental problems are dark, dirty, and rare. They aren't, but an old specter persists that these are character defects . . .

From the vantage point of many clinicians, people who seek psychotherapy are often the last people who should hide. In a society as pressured and depersonalizing as ours, psychotherapists often serve as the "confidants" of the community. Of far greater concern to the administrator should well be the staff member who doesn't take stock of personal habits, professional attitudes, and interpersonal conflicts. People in therapy give thought in disciplined ways to their professional and social relationships. They stop to consider the ethical bases of their endeavors, their motivations, and their health. Many professional people spend time and money to guarantee that their lives and jobs have meaning.

By contrast, the individual who does not give careful consideration to the quality of his or her life might be the employee meriting concern. This is not to say that everyone needs or would benefit from psychotherapy or that the only way to lead a disciplined life is to take time for therapy. However, myths about psychotherapy deter those who would like to be in therapy but wouldn't dare for fear of how treatment might be interpreted.

Many outstanding citizens have benefited from therapy—privately.

"I'm sure I'm the only one at my firm who's in therapy," states Manuel, a dignified accountant.

"And how do you know this?" his therapist asks, knowing that several of his colleagues are currently in psychoanalysis.

"Well, nobody ever *talks* about being in therapy," he replies. "So people must think it's something only troubled people do."

Although the therapist takes Manuel's comments seriously, she knows better.

According to the National Institute of Mental Health, 20 percent of all people are affected by depression. Twenty-five percent of all employer paid medical claims are for psychotherapeutic interventions. People in therapy seek to find ways to make their personal and work lives maximally fulfilling. These people don't want the stresses we all share to impinge on their productivity.

There are a number of reasons why people around the world are shy about sharing the fact that they are in therapy. First, modern psychotherapy is a relatively new field. All cultures and civilizations have endorsed the science of folk remedies or *physical* medicine. Whether it's the doctor of a tribal village chanting incantations or the modern physician prescribing penicillin, the art and science of physical health has been respected throughout history. However, the art and science of mental health is still poorly understood.

Second, many of the psychiatric patients of the past were typically mentally disabled. Treated through physical interventions including surgery and crude medications, the mentally tormented were herded into overly crowded institutions. Before the discovery of antipsychotic drugs, the truly "mentally ill" were often wrapped in sheets and confined to dehumanizing hospital wards.

These are not the types of individuals most commonly seen by modern therapists. If people assume that only "sick" people see psychotherapists, they are out of step with modern life. Of course, some people still suffer severe forms of mental disability such as schizophrenia. Fortunately, many of these individuals are now able—with the help of medications and community support—to lead gratifying lives. They are the minority of people in modern therapy.

Most clients are dealing with adjustment issues, anxiety, or depression. Many are disappointed with the quality of their lives. Whether living in high rise buildings, the suburbs, or small towns, many feel alienated and unprepared for the anonymity of their lives. They turn to professionals for guidance.

People who seek therapy demand mastery over their lives and careers. Intelligent and psychologically resourceful, they want solutions. Neither sick nor sinister, people in therapy are participating in a relatively new and entirely honest mechanism for growth and self review. Unlike some of their co-workers who might deny their inner conflicts, they prefer to face life's challenges in constructive ways.

Why are people so secretive about their psychotherapeutic ventures? Why must they hide "therapy" from supervisors and bosses? Proud and deserving respect, dare they not tarnish their records by admitting that, like everybody else, they are human and therefore vulnerable? Personal pride is valuable.

Few self-respecting people want to be misrepresented or unfairly criticized when in fact they are living the self-examined life.

For these reasons, the attitudes of employers, administrators, and bosses must be updated. Some have already begun their education. Large corporations are beginning to offer training sessions for supervisors and special assistance to employees who need therapy. If a staff person is in treatment, an employer may assume that this person is resourceful and very serious about the quality of his or her work and life.

Executives and administrators seek psychotherapy, too, but they rarely talk about it at work. No one does.

Whereas some groups of colleagues and friends openly discuss their personal lives, others never utter a self-revealing word. People have a legitimate right to privacy. However, if people need to sneak down halls, evade questions, and apologize if therapy visits are "discovered," our places of employment cannot claim to be "safe places."

Whether you are an employer or an employee, you may need to review your knowledge about who really goes to therapy and what goes on there.

THE RISK OF RUSHED DICHOTOMIES

A tendency to dichotomize pervades the attitudes of many citizens. At times we think too fast and too little about complex ideas. One result of this rushed non-reflectiveness is the oversimplification of subtle issues and an inclination to think in terms of opposites: "sick and healthy," "good and bad," "strong and weak." For many, this "either-or" mentality serves a self-protective function. By talking and thinking in terms of good and bad opposites, some people believe they can get on the "good side." As long as either-or people affirm that they are on the "right" (healthy, popular, competent, stable) track, they feel secure and beyond judgment. They forget that we are all on the same ship. Just as there are many shades of honesty, competence, and physical health and beauty, so there are many types of mental stability. Colleagues and friends are all coping with similar issues—at different times, in different ways, and in different degrees.

The important questions for an employer to ask should *not* be: "Is she or he in psychotherapy, and if so, for what?" Instead, the administrator should ask: "Is this person performing the required tasks of his or her job? If not, what is he or she doing about it? Is our work environment one that fosters personal and professional growth? If not, what can we do to ensure optimal motivation in our workplace?"

Successful administrators inspire, listen, and win cooperation. They are able to channel employees' energies in maximally productive directions. Able to cope constructively with conflict, gifted administrators are self aware. Talented supervisors don't let their personal limitations dilute their productivity. Knowing they will be given a fair hearing, employees openly discuss their strengths and liabilities with these kinds of leaders.

Most people who seek therapy—whether administrators or employees—strive for the characteristics I have emphasized. William Cutler, a thirty-six-year-old executive who became a psychotherapy client and marathon runner after a painful divorce, stated it very well: "I want to be a winner: a winner on the track, a winner on the job, and a winner in *life*."

CHAPTER 12

A NOTE
TO THE PERSON
IN THERAPY

> *Knowledge*
> > *comes . . .*
> *Wisdom*
> > *lingers . . .*

Alfred, Lord Tennyson

Most people, after completing therapy, become more self-assured, more open, and more honest with their parents, partners and friends. If your loved ones ask you questions that are stimulated by this book, I hope that you will respond as candidly as possible. This will be your opportunity to bring clarity and directness to the little-known and, to some people, frightening concept of psychotherapy.

Although therapy may have become a familiar process for you, it still remains a mystery to many people. Your parents or partners may have found other ways to survive and, hopefully, thrive. Some of your friends may seem to sail along without searching for answers to the kinds of questions that bothered you. Despite your openness in other areas, you may feel shy about telling employers, employees, and colleagues that you are in therapy. Although thousands of people seek growth through therapy and self-help groups, some critics still view these processes as self-centered or trendy. For your sake, I have tried to clear up the distortions. You deserve respect for your sophisticated efforts to live fully.

Since you want to live wisely, I hope you will share your new insights with relatives and friends. Mysteries and misunderstandings surround the therapy process. Because of the need for confidentiality in our work, we clinicians must be silent about the people with whom we've met all day. We are unable to describe the dramas that fill our hours and the thought we give to each unique situation. To some, we may appear to be quiet, reflective, or "tight-lipped." Thus we, too, participate in creating the mystery which shrouds the therapeutic process.

You also bear responsibility for the mystique and misconceptions. When a person is deeply involved in therapy, a self-reflective, internal re-processing preoccupies the mind. Although this is a sign of active engagement to your therapist, your silence may baffle relatives and friends.

"I liked you better before you started therapy," Patty said to her partner.

"But *why?*" asked Paul, feeling hurt and misunderstood.

"You were more fun; you weren't *thinking* all the time," responded Patty. "You tell your therapist more than you tell me."

"Oh," said Paul quietly. Once again, withdrawing into thoughtful reflection.

If your friends are resentful of your new preoccupation, your parents or partners may feel even more alienated. There is a lot that people don't know about therapy. Parents and partners worry that they'll be unfairly represented when you talk about them. Threatened by your increasing independence, they may fear your rejection. If you're lucky, your parents respect you for your therapeutic gains. Nevertheless, they may wonder, at times, whether your problems are their fault. They may ask why therapy is taking so long. Stumbling, they often ask (or harbor) questions that you aren't ready to answer. In this book, I have tried to assist you by responding to the questions parents, partners, or peers ask when their loved ones in therapy seek privacy.

Learning to know, love, and respect yourself is a common therapy goal for you. For your loved ones, your therapy may be a different kind of challenge. Your mother may ask herself if she failed you, and your father may assume he should have spent more time with you. Although some of their conclusions may be partially correct, parents or partners often punish themselves needlessly. Or, in reviewing their own lives, they may focus on irrelevant "wrongs." When people lack information, they become the victims of fantasy. The truth, although it may hurt at first, is far better than false assumptions and confusion.

At just the time when you begin to attain clarity, parents or partners often feel defensive. They don't want to intrude on you but they are curious. If vulnerable, they may cringe at any hint of disapproval from you. If defensive, they may criticize you, your therapist, or the therapy process. I have written this book to help you, to help them, and to help your friends break through the silence. I hope that as you begin to communicate more openly with loved ones, you will be able to describe your thoughts clearly—without blaming or shaming.

It's your job to claim responsibility for your life—whatever your special challenges may be. It is your loved ones' job, as I have said often, to claim responsibility for *their* lives—past, present, and future.

What your parents, partners or friends may not realize is that you do not want to criticize them but you do want to attain mastery over your own unique life challenges. Many parents, for instance, are unaware of their adult sons' and daughters' continued yearnings for appreciation. Many partners do not know or understand the complex formative events which their loved ones experienced. Like you, your loved ones yearn for love and respect. After reading this book, they may be able to appreciate their own efforts in child-rearing or in a relationship, in spite of their "mistakes." Isn't this, after all, one of *your* therapeutic goals? The more we can accept ourselves in spite of our imperfections, the more caring we can be towards each other. As we become emotionally honest and open about ourselves, relationships deepen.

If and when you are ready, you will convey who you really are with simplicity and freedom. Until then, I hope this book will lessen and soften the silent spaces between you and those you love.

NOTES

1. "Unite and Conquer," an article in the February 5, 1990 issue of *Newsweek* lists the following numbers for self-help clearinghouses:

> *National Self-Help Clearinghouse (212) 642-2944*
> *California Self-Help Center (310) 825-1799*
> *Massachusetts Clearinghouse of Mutual Help Groups*
> *(413) 545-2313*

These clearinghouses will be able to offer you the locations, phone numbers, and goals of many types of self-help groups. As stated in the *Newsweek* article, "Support groups in the past few years seem to have sorted themselves into three basic categories: those that address problems of addictive behavior (Compulsive Shoppers, Workaholics and others that often follow a slight variation of AA's twelve steps); those for dealing with a transition or some other crisis (Widowed Persons Service, Recently Divorced Catholics); and those for friends and relatives of people with problems (Adult Children of Alcoholics, Parents of Agoraphobic Teenagers).

2. *The Directory of Self-Help Support Groups* compiled in 1993 by the Self-Help Clearinghouse of Greater Washington, D.C. offers hundreds of national listings and phone numbers for supportive and self-help services throughout America. For information about your specific concerns, you may order this Directory or request information by writing or calling:

> *The Mental Health Association of Northern Virginia*
> *7630 Little River Turnpike, Suite 206*
> *Annandale, Virginia 22003*
> *(703) 941-LINK*

REFERENCES

"Drug Abuse and Dependence." *The Harvard Medical School Newsletter* Oct. 1989: 1-4.

Ehrenberg, O. and M. Ehrenberg. *The Psychotherapy Maze: A Consumer's Guide to Getting In and Out of Therapy.* New York: Simon & Schuster, 1975.

"Family Therapy—Part II." *The Harvard Medical School Newsletter* May 1988: 1-3.

Forward, Susan. *Toxic Parents.* New York: Bantam, 1989.

Guralnik, D. *Webster's New World Dictionary.* New York: Simon & Schuster, 1984.

Littwin, S. *The Postponed Generation: Why American Youth Are Growing Up Later.* New York: William Morrow and Company, 1986.

McCarthy, Coleman. "The Last Closet." *The Washington Post* 4 Aug. 1988.

McIntosh, J. *Passages Journal.* Philadelphia: Running Press Books, 1986.

O'Kane, Monica L. *Hey, Mom, I'm Home Again! Strategies for Parents and Grown Children Who Live Together.* Saint Paul, MN: Marlor Press, Inc., 1992.

Okimoto, Jean and Phyllis Stegall. *The Boomerang Kids: How to Live with Adult Children Who Return Home.* Canada: Little, Brown, 1987.

Peck, M. S. *The Road Less Traveled*. New York: Simon & Schuster, 1978.

Roth, S. *Psychotherapy: The Art of Wooing Nature*. New Jersey: Jason Aronson, 1987.

Scarff, Maggie. *Intimate Partners*. New York: Random House, 1987.

Toffler, Alvin. *A Mother's Journal*. Philadelphia: Running Press, 1985.

"Unite and Conquer." *Newsweek* 5 Feb. 1990: 55.

Vine, Phyllis. *Families in Pain*. New York: Pantheon Books, 1982.

Viorst, Judith. *Necessary Losses*. New York: Simon & Schuster, 1986.